IT'S *still* ALL ABOUT ENERGY

VOLUME 2

OTHER WORK BY CARI MOFFET:

It's All About Energy: A Beginner's Guide to Accessing your Energetic SUPERPOWER Physically, Personally, and Professionally

IT'S *still* ALL ABOUT ENERGY

VOLUME 2

A Guide to Accessing Your Energetic SUPERPOWER through Life, Death, and Bits in Between

CARI MOFFET

Cover Design: @Fay Thompson of Big Moose Publishing
Published by: Big Moose Publishing
PO Box 127 Site 601 RR#6 Saskatoon, SK CANADA S7K3J9
www.bigmoosepublishing.com

Because of the dynamic nature of the Internet, any web addresses or links contained in this book may have changed since publication and may no longer be valid. The views expressed in this work are solely those of the author and do not necessarily reflect the views of the publisher, and the publisher hereby disclaims any responsibility for them.

The author of this book does not dispense medical advice or prescribe the use of any technique as a form of treatment for physical, emotional, or medical problems without the advice of a physician, either directly or indirectly. The intent of the author is only to offer information of a general nature to help you in your quest for emotional and spiritual well-being. In the event you use any of the information in this book for yourself, which is your constitutional right, the author and the publisher assume no responsibility for your actions.

ISBN: 978-1-989840-72-6 (sc)
ISBN: 978-1-989840-73-3 (ebook)

Big Moose Publishing 05/2024

DEDICATION

To my grandparents who have taught me so much about physical life and spiritual death. I miss you.

I want to also dedicate this book to my four amazing nephews. If I had chosen to have children, I would want them to be exactly like you (scary hey):

Steele, you have embodied the family gene of strength and resilience. It's okay to rely on others when you get tired. I admire you for your inner power.

Sterling, you are more talented in speaking and acting than you may ever realize. I admire you for going after your dreams and what brings you joy.

Beckett, your brain power and charisma will take you wherever you want to go in life. I admire you for your faith and your love for humanity and family.

Quinn, your kindness and ability to figure things out will be your superpower in life. Pursue what brings you happiness. I admire you for your willingness to help others.

It has been a pleasure watching you all grow up and discover more of who you are. You make me want to be a better auntie, a better human.

Big embarrassing auntie kisses in public for you all!!!

CONTENTS

PREFACE

This book has been divinely inspired. What if we allowed divine intervention to lead our lives all the time? What if we moved through life, intuitively feeling our way and not ever judging our decisions or holding ourselves back because of what others think? I can hardly even imagine that in my mind, yet I desire it with my heart.

As I sit down to write the words my soul is longing to say, my mind wants to shut it down and distract me with outside noise or even a nap. I am a master at distraction and wonder. If there were no distractions, what I would have created by now. I will not dwell on that but rather carry on.

Disclaimer: Some of you will not agree with everything you read in this book. That's okay! Allow that to be okay for yourself. We can still be friends. No one on the planet believes everything you do either – for real! So, take what you can and discard the rest and thank you for reading another human's point of view.

Also, as I pieced together these writings from the last four years, I realized how much the world has changed. You will read about some of my struggles with Covid and what it taught me. Living through a (so called) pandemic brought many things to the surface. It's also interesting how we forget how traumatized we all were being forced into a fearful existence. Many of us just choose to forget these times: the segregation and loss of friends and family who think differently may just be too much to face now it is all over.

What a crazy time and the 'crazy' seems to have not stopped since. You see it, you can feel it, and experience it. I wonder if this is because we are preparing for a new way to exist. Are things finally being brought into the open so that we can experience a better life on the planet? Old ideas, systems and beliefs must be crushed and buried as new ways of doing things are born, if not for us, possibly for the generations to come.

Also in this book, you will read about three significant deaths in my life. Death is a part of life, but no one really talks about it. Even at funerals or celebrations of life, people rarely talk about their own mortality. Are we really celebrating? No, we are likely mourning and saying good-bye. Is it appropriate to celebrate? I will explore a bit of this from my own life.

It is because of people like you, who pick up a book like

this, who are tapping into their own growth and awareness, that contribute to the creation of the energy of the planet to shift.

Something that I did not mention in my first book (*It's All About Energy)* is to buy a new journal just for reading these books. Answer the questions at the end of each chapter. The growth you will experience will be intense (if you so dare). You can also read through the book and finish it like a race, but you will likely not receive all you can from its offerings.

With that said, keep on uncovering the truth in your life, keep seeking answers, keep finding ways to evolve into your higher consciousness. This is likely why we are here, and why you chose (yes chose) to come back to the planet to have an experience.

Through life, through death, and all the bits in between, there is energy.

PROLOGUE

In the process of writing of this book, I went on a writing retreat with my friend, Patricia Meier, at the Dakota Dunes resort. The resort is situated on the Whitecap Dakota Nation land. We decided this place was the perfect place to work on our next books and catch up on life.

As I looked out on the snowy horizon from my well-appointed room, I asked the Dakota land to support me and what I came here to do. You may not be aware, but all energy around you, land included, can support and contribute to you. You just need to ask. And so, I did. I wanted to finish writing this book and I am notorious for being distracted and wasting my time. I see squirrels everywhere! I felt the land was listening, and did feel its guidance to help me get the job done.

Patricia and I enjoyed our time at this resort. I managed to get the majority of my book written and even had time to play and enjoy amazing food. When it came time to leave, something unexplainable took over me.

I had been exploring fear of doing something big in my life, such as writing a second book and launching an online program. It seemed daunting and a bit scary. It's putting yourself out there for all to see and possibly judge. The fear that I was experiencing spilled over into my drive home. My fear while driving seemed to match the fear that men of the land had held. These two energies appeared to vibrate the same and exploded when they met each other. All of a sudden, I was scared to go home, to travel in this cold. This was unlike me.

I live in Saskatchewan, Canada, and usually at least one week of the year in winter we have a deep freeze, and we were smack in it. All I could picture was my vehicle breaking down and me freezing to death. I contemplated staying another night so that the temperature could warm up from -36°C to -30°C the next day. My husband talked me out of it and said to just come home. "If the truck starts, just come home."

Well, the truck started. It didn't like it too much, but it turned over. I was bundled up in my warmest jacket, boots, toque, mitts and scarf – only my eyes were showing. I hugged Patricia good-bye, and we went our separate ways. She had no fear. Why did I?

My shoulders were up to my ears trying to stay warm. I couldn't decide if my ass was frozen or burning from the seat warmer as it felt so strange. I could feel every bump in the road as the suspension of the truck was next to nothing. My windshield from the inside began to frost up as I talked to myself. "Damn, I can't see." I reached back to grab my scraper to get the frost off. "Why do we live here?" I wondered, as I cursed my ancestors for their migration.

The fear continued for about 30 more minutes as I drove past six dead vehicles on the side of the road.

"Why am I so scared? I have a blanket. It's daylight. I even have a candle and some food and water. It's not my time to die," I thought to myself.

These thoughts and a conversation at breakfast made mc realize the power of fear. While enjoying our meal, we talked about the atrocities that the indigenous people have endured over history. There is something called the 'Starlight Tours', where our officers of the law would drive indigenous people out into the land (some even had their shoes and jackets taken), and they would leave them out there to find their way back. Many would die. This was their punishment for being the 'troublemakers' of the city. I couldn't imagine the fear they must have endured. These are human beings being treated as 'less than' and in ways that no other human would want to endure.

Was my subconscious picking up on this? I wanted to deny it. I wanted to even deny the entire story as it's so horrendous and heartbreaking.

"Really, how can my consciousness and body be feeling this?!"

I filled up for gas again, since I didn't want to go below half a tank, and got back on the road. I noticed my body was so sore and in pain. I'm not sure if it was from holding my posture to stay warm or from the bumpy ride or from my brain showing me this story. It hurt.

I began to have tears in my eyes. My heart hurt for these people who have frozen to their death and for all the humans who have been mistreated. The acknowledgment was real in my body. I cried for them. They were silent tears, as I was too afraid to let them flow. If I did break down, my eyes would freeze shut in just a moment.

I drove another hour and my body did not feel good. I thought I was going to vomit, and my head was hurting. "What is this now? Am I getting a migraine? I don't understand. Body, what are you trying to tell me?"

I filled up again for gas and found some Advil and ginger ale. My truck was warm now. The heartbreak feeling had left, and my body was starting to recover. I made it home and felt rather well. I even noticed the beauty of the trees, snow, and the bright sky as it held everything together.

The next day I pondered what had happened on my drive home. Could my body really have picked up the fear, the pain, the sorrow of the land and some of its history? As my energy gets clearer to realize that I (we) are a part of it all, there is no doubt that this could be. I did ask for contributions of the land. How was this contributing to my greatest good?

I went to sit in my sauna and think on this. As my body began to sweat it felt like tears coming out of me. I am notorious for hanging on to people's pain and hardships. For some reason, my body thinks that is its job. I released it of its job and told it "I am safe." I told myself that I no longer must hold the pain of others. I am to acknowledge it, be aware of it, and leave it be. Do not pick it up.

With regards to our horrid history, I feel there is nothing I can do today other than remember and do what I can to not allow the mistreatment of other humans. I choose to live in total acceptance and love for humanity regardless of race, religion, skin color, differences of opinion, etc. Only today matters for a better tomorrow. We can remember the past, but it won't serve us to live there. We all must learn from it, forgive, and move on to create a highly anticipated 'New Earth'.

PART 1

LIFE

Be yourself; everyone else is already taken.

- Oscar Wilde

CHAPTER 1

I DON'T WANT TO BE HERE, OR DO I?

I can't tell you when I first had this feeling of not wanting to be here… on this planet. I think I was a child. I wondered why I was born here, living, and breathing, trying to get through life. Those are serious thoughts for someone in elementary school. It possibly started on my actual day of birth. I didn't want to come out. I gave my mom a severely hard time (which she reminds me of every year)! I should have been birthed by C-section, but they pulled me out eventually, kicking and screaming, a 10 pound babe to be exact. Why didn't I want to come out?

Maybe I didn't want to have a physical body and a human experience. Maybe I was second guessing my choice to have a life on the planet. Maybe this is why there are so many unexplained miscarriages. Maybe?

During the horrible Covid days, I had two friends who struggled with the virus and were in the hospital. They called out for help amongst their energy friends, and I caught myself saying to both friends, "Do you want to be here? Choose and your body will respond." They chose to stay, and they both recovered. I even remember thinking, "Cari, you can't say that to someone." Well, it's true. If you want to stay, be here; if you don't, there will be ways provided for your exit.

I prayed for an exit in my 20s. After my separation from my first husband, I was alone, afraid, angry and depressed. To this day, that was the darkest night of my soul and it lasted for much longer than a night. I remember driving over a bridge in the city I lived at the time and just praying that a car would swerve over the line and hit me. I was lost and wanted a way out. I was not brave enough to take myself out, but if someone else wanted to, I would be open to that. I wanted an exit.

A couple decades later, I was taking an online class. The teacher said, "How many of you have chosen to be here with all conviction? On a scale of 1-10 (10 being high) how committed are you to living on earth?" Oh my gosh, I'm only a 5! She went on to say, "Can you commit today to being fully here and stepping into who you are, and realizing that you chose to come to earth to have its experiences and deal with your karma? Can you fully commit to being here?"

"What the heck, Cari," I questioned myself. I just told two friends to decide if they wanted to be here and live, and here I am, half-assing it, not sure still, at nearly 50 years of age, if I want to be here! "What kind of life am I attracting by just having those thoughts in my head? I'm not fully here! I'm not here! I want to be here. I choose to be here. I choose to be here on earth fully. I step into my power, and I AM HERE!"

A few months after writing these thoughts down about death and being here, I had another experience with my husband with the exact same theme. (Pay close attention to when there are three or more instances that are all the same theme in your life!)

I was nursing him all week with some digestive difficulties. Covid made a lot of us avoid the hospital, but I was very close to admitting him. One particularly difficult night, I asked him the same question, "Do you want to be here?" I honestly was expecting a "no". I was expecting to put on a brave face to honor that decision, but he said "yes".

I started doing some energy work on him as there was an incredibly strong hold pulling him to the other side. I found myself cutting energetic cords between him and his mother who had passed. She ironically died from digestive complications nearly 5 years to the day in the same city as we were in. It was a strange coincidence, but if we had not made those connections, I may not have known where to look to release the energy pull.

I stayed up late praying and doing energy work over his body as we agreed if he was still feeling this way in the morning, he would be going to the hospital. I wouldn't have been able to stay with him because of the (crazy/stupid/dumb) rules of the pandemic.

I remember the visions of Jesus assisting me. I remember his mom's image vanishing.

We woke the next day. He had slept a lot of the night. His first few words were, "I am feeling better today than I have in a long time." Whoa, and yay, and whew!!! This experience really did feel like an 'out' for him if he wanted it. He chose to stay. We asked for help, we cut some energetic ties, and then we gave thanks. There were some tears here. It was a like a contract renewal to continue our lives together on this planet.

I wonder if these potential exit points come along in life to make us recommit to being here on the planet. I have heard other teachings say we have 7 exit points in life where we can choose to stay or go. They say cats have nine lives and so maybe we have seven?

Are you fully here? Do you choose to be here?

"Guides, angels, ancestors, help me to be fully here. Help

me to remember why I so desperately wanted to come here. Show me my purpose and reason to live this earthly life in this physical body."

This is my prayer. Maybe it's yours. Is it time to be fully here?

Recently, I was at a funeral. I went to support my friend who lost his mom. These are always moments to remember that time is short, and it won't be forever. As Andy Dufresne says in my husband's favorite movie, The Shawshank Redemption, "You either get busy living or you get busy dying." This really is true. Time's a ticking!

Thoughts to Ponder:

1. On a scale of 1-10 (10 is high and fully committed), how committed are you to being here?

2. Have you ever recognized your exit points? I wonder what prompted you to stay.

3. Are you ready to fully commit to yourself and your greatness, and trust your decision to be on this planet?

CHAPTER 2

COLLECTING THE PIECES

Does it ever feel like you are not all here? Where did you go?

Years ago, my colleague and friend, Fay, led me in a meditation of picking up the pieces of you that you've left behind. Spirituality was a very new concept for me at the time. Religion was all I knew and it's extremely different from spirituality. She led us into our past through meditation, and we looked for places and relationships where we had possibly left parts of ourselves.

I know, this seems really silly, because you are right here right now. Where else could you be?

After studying and observing energy, it's super simple for

me to see that we leave part of our energetic selves behind in different situations, personal connections and even places.

I'm sure you all know someone who reminisces about the past a bit too much. They love living there. They connect to those times. Possibly someone they loved was lost there. It's where they want to live, because it was where they were all together (likely in more ways than one). They keep going there because a part of them is still there energetically.

What about a place or city that you really enjoyed and connected to and didn't want to come home? You felt complete in these places. Gosh, I have had a few of those. The first time I did this meditation, New York was coming up. It was back in the early 2000s that my husband and I travelled there. The vibe was amazing! We saw ball games and shows. We went to a specialty spa, ate at fantastic restaurants, saw famous landmarks, and made out in Central Park (yeah, quit judging). It was super fun, and I loved every second. I left a part of me there because it was so me – carefree, fun, and vibrant. I called it back. It didn't need to still be there. I wanted all pieces of me here and now. I have pictures to remember the experience. I don't need to keep part of my energetic self there.

Then there is trauma/drama. Not to make light of anything anyone has gone through, but these are wicked times on our energy system. Whether it's full-blown drama with family or friends or abusive trauma or tragic events, these all play a massive part on our energy system. There are huge pieces of us that sometimes get left behind, because we don't know what else to do with the event. We may even physically walk away and leave, scarred by the exchange or what we witnessed.

Recently I was working with a client who wanted help with her energy system. She could feel when people attacked her energetically. She had an incredibly traumatic up bringing, one that I don't know if I could have endured to be honest. She has such strength in choosing to be here now after all she has gone through. As I was guiding her through activities to make her energetic system stronger, we got stuck on parts of her that may have been missing. When I say that, it's only in the energetic sense. "Did you leave parts of yourself in that abusive relationship, the abandonment of your childhood, the suicide of your family member and friend?" How could you not, especially if you are unaware that this is even a thing.

I wonder if it's possibly, that in being such an empath, she didn't know what else to do in the moment, and so she gave a piece of herself as an offering to smooth things over? I'm not sure if or why we are doing this. Maybe we just are not aware of it happening. It was time to gather up her pieces and maybe it is for you as well. I led her in the following short meditation. Feel free to do this on your own as you sit and read this.

Meditation for Collecting the Pieces

Get as comfortable as you can. Take a couple deep breaths and really settle in to your surroundings. Ask your guides, angels, God, universe, etc. to be with you and to show you what you need to look at for your highest good.

Ask your highest self to show you where in your life you left a piece of you behind. Allow the vision to come. Don't force it. The first thing you are shown is the right thing. Have a look at it. You don't have to stay there. Just tell it, "You can come back to me now." Just stay aware to what is happening in the body.

Ask again, "Is there any other place that I left myself behind or am living in the past?" If you are shown another place, take a look and say, "You can come back to me now."

Keep doing this until you are not shown anything else. Breathe and be present in your body. It may respond to your spirit coming back. Just allow whatever is happening to happen. There is no judgment here of right or wrong. This just is.

When you feel like this is complete, come back to the space you are in.

When I completed this meditation with my client, she

opened her eyes and said "Wow." She felt as though her body was puffing up to blow up a balloon. She felt it expanding but not really expanding. She was coming back to herself.

There is one more piece to this that may or may not resonate with you. If you believe in past lives, do you think it's possible to leave some of yourself there? If your race, gender, or beliefs have forced you to be someone else, do you believe you may have left some of yourself behind? These are also places to call yourself back.

When you fully choose to be here in whatever year you are reading this book, and you ask for all parts of you to return so that you can live fully here, you are stronger energetically than most people on the planet. We live in this world of oblivion. It's time to be more aware. It was Jesus that said, "I come to give you life and to give you life abundantly." Walking around only partly here and with a feeling of not wanting to live is not abundant. There is more for us.

Thoughts to Ponder:

1. Do you feel complete or is it possible that parts of you have been left in relationships, situations or even places?

2. Call back this energy for yourself. Take time to do the meditation. Imagine living a life where you are fully present, with no part of you left behind.

CHAPTER 3

THE ENERGY OF GETTING CLEAR

The greatest thing you can do for your life is knowing what you want and getting clear. When I started my massage business, I put on the intake form, "What would you like to see happen today with your health?" I found it very interesting how people do not think of what they want or know they have the power to change things in their body by choosing something different. Many people go about life just accepting what comes instead of creating what they want, need or desire.

Pick something in your life right now that you would like to see happen. Basically, ask yourself, "What do I want?" If you are really daring, ask yourself, "If I had that, what would that give me?" See if you can ask yourself these questions 7 times: "If I had that, what would it give me?" Then, you will really know what you want and why. Sometimes it's much different that you realize. Here's an example of what I mean.

I really want my office building to sell. (And if I had that, what would that give me?) I would have a huge chunk of money in my account. (And if that happens what would that give me?) Freedom to do more of what I love and not what I need to do. (And if you had that, what would I have?) More fun and joy in my life. (And if I had that, what would I have?) A life that vibrates high. (And if I had that, what would I have?) Opportunities and abundance would be attracted to me. (And if I had that, what would I have?) Freedom to do what I want when I want and with whom I want.

Interesting. That is likely why I want to sell my office building, to have the freedom to do what I want, when I want and with whom I want. Who doesn't want that?!

When you discover the real 'want', make that your mantra to help you manifest. For example, more of what I desire will come from "I want the freedom to do what I want when I want and with whom I want" versus "I want to sell my office building." You can also be creative in reminding yourself of your mantra. Maybe put on a piece of jewelry that you can easily see (ring or bracelet), or paint a finger nail a different color, or put sticky notes up in your home and office. These are effective daily reminders of what you really want. Of course, a reminder or alarm on your phone will work too.

When you know what you want, you start to stand in your power and watch the universe deliver it to you. Most times we do not know the 'how is this ever going to happen.' Here lies the lesson in trust. I believe it could possibly be the hardest lesson to learn.

How do I sit here and just trust this will happen? I know what I want, but I have no idea how this will transpire. Do you really have to know?

It's not that you should sit back and wait for it to fall onto your lap. You must be proactive too. If no one knows my building is for sale, then how does it sell? Obviously, I must advertise and put it out there. When a buyer comes, I must work with them and negotiate. I can't just sit on my butt and hope everything goes through. I must engage. You see what I'm saying?

There is mystery and divine timing in this world that we may not understand. When you put your request out to the universe/God/creator, do you trust that it is being heard and things are lining up for your greatest good? Trust is so massive. This is where you feel like you are doing nothing. How do you trust the unknown?

I want you to think back to a time in your life when you were in trouble. Maybe it was financial, or a relationship gone wrong or a time when you just needed help. What happened? Are you okay now? Get what I'm saying? It worked itself out. When we are in the thick of stress, we cannot see how it's ever going to work out. This is the same when you are manifesting something and now you need to trust. You have no idea how it's going to work itself out, and you don't need to. Your only job is to know what you want and then trust you will receive.

Thoughts to Ponder:

1. Write out what you really want.
2. Play the game of 7 questions: If I received that, what would it give me?
3. Write out your real desire for what you want.
4. Remember the last time you were stressed and how it worked out. Feel that trust in your body and start to believe the universe is lining things up for you now that you are clear on your desires.

CHAPTER 4

TRUSTING YOUR INTUITION

How do we ever develop the feeling of trust? How do we trust anyone or even life itself? Portions of this book have been written during the pandemic of 2020. It was the perfect time to explore this issue as we faced these questions daily: Who do you trust? Who is telling the truth?

The media and big pharma were being questioned. People who we deemed as safe to trust were telling us a different narrative than we once believed. Who do we trust? This was all becoming confusing as we could find supporting arguments to support whatever we wanted to believe in. This is true with many things today.

Did we have better news sources in years past and so we trusted them to be the truth? I'm thinking about our nightly news. Or were we just so naïve that we believed them to be the truth (because they would never lie to us). Now, we are waking up to the real truth (maybe we have been fed a narrative to benefit certain groups of people)?

I remember one day posting on social media my agreement to an opinion and receiving two nasty responses from a past co-worker and a family member. I was shocked, but not surprised, as we were all trying to find our own truth. My cousin found a document that supported the exact opposite stance to what I agreed with. Which document do we trust?

What if it didn't come down to a document at all? What if trust came down to something deeper within us? What if trust was trusting ourselves and that was all that mattered?

Do you trust yourself? What does that even mean? Do you have a sense of knowing or a feeling that tells you what to do and how to do it because you trust your senses?

We have these senses deep within us. I'm talking about the Clairs: Clairsentience (clear feeling), Clairaudience (clear hearing), Claircognizance (clear knowing), Clairvoyance (clear seeing). These are the most popular ones. This is your intuition.

Your intuition is a part of you that has been forgotten. The untapped, most important part of you that many of us do not use! If you start strengthening your intuition, your senses will give you the messages of trust, and so much more.

Some of you are going to say that you trust God. That is fine. How do you hear/sense/see/feel what God is saying? This is your intuition (the way you receive the guidance), your higher power, your 6th sense.

Likely no one has even told you that you are intuitive, that you too have these abilities. Maybe you do know this part of you is available to access, but then how do you trust this inborn ability to know? How do you find your way back to your intuitive powers and be able to trust?

My strongest sense is claircognizance, the sense of knowing. I know what I know even though I don't know how I know! I have used this sense for years and I trust it. I trust this part of me. It is not the logical mind that gives me the messages. It literally comes from the opposite side of our brain. I cannot recall the first time it made its appearance. I was likely a child and then just kept working with it, not really knowing what I was doing. When things started becoming true (for example: that person's a jerk, and I knew it, but wasn't shown it, but then they proved it) I trusted my sense of knowing even more.

I do recall a time when I was about 16, and I was at a concert in our church. The group was from Edmonton, Alberta, Canada, and called Morning Star. I knew one person in the group. They were amazing to my 16-year-old brain. I wanted to do that. They trained for the summer, recorded two albums and toured Canada for a year just singing and playing and sharing. I guess you could say it was a calling. Who was calling? Intuition? God? My soul? Or are all these the same thing? I did listen and ended up doing the exact same thing just two years later. I trusted the sense of knowing that "this is what I want to do when I'm done high school." My sense of knowing knew this would be fun for me. And it was!

Years later my sense of knowing led me to massage college. I knew this was what I wanted. Here is where my intuition really showed its true colors. I had never had a professional massage in my life. Yet, there I was, first day of classes, ready to become a massage therapist. I did have a slight panic attack when I realized that I may hate this course. I moved to a new city, got a student loan, and transferred a part time job to my new city, all in aspirations to go to a full time private massage college. How did I know I would even like it? Thank goodness I trusted my intuition. I loved it and sustained an abnormally long career as a therapist.

In each of these major life stories, I'm glad I trusted my claircognizance. It was there, available, and easy to access. This sense of knowing is a part of me and so it's also easy to trust. In this entire world, I trust myself the most. Anything outside of you is more difficult to trust as you may not receive the same reliable guidance as your 6th sense.

I'm sure every person who reads these pages has been hurt by someone they trusted. We are all humans and mess up. No one is perfect. Therefore, it is slightly harder to trust others than ourselves, and so important to start to play with your own 'clair'.

Many people use meditation, quietness, stillness, journaling, etc. to get to a place of calm to hear this voice within. Others will find a psychic to help them receive messages as intuition is their specialty. When we rely on psychics, we miss the opportunity to discover our own unique gifts. We all have this ability within us. Some just choose to ignore, and others cannot create the space to listen.

Start to play with this intuition. The next time you hear your phone ring or buzz, ask yourself, who is contacting me? See them, hear them, know it's them, feel them and then check your phone to confirm if you were right. It's okay if you were wrong too. Just keep playing. If you go to a hotel, play with the room number you will be given. Use your intuition to try and figure it out before you check in. Use your intuition to know which elevator will arrive first. Keep playing. Keep it light and fun and you will start to develop a deeper part of yourself that you may have forgotten.

Thoughts to Ponder:

1. Do you know your greatest 'clair' to receive messages (feeling, seeing, knowing, hearing)?

2. Is there a problem or concern in your life that you could use your intuition to figure it out?

3. Do you trust your intuition or something/someone else to figure your life out for you?

CHAPTER 5

SEPARATION

As I'm sitting down to write this, we are inching our way out of this 'pandemic' in 2021. I'm not sure if we are in for something more after they lift all restrictions or not. Time will tell. It's been quite a ride. I don't even want to write about it, or talk about it, since we have been consumed with it for 15 months now. We have talked about the same topic daily for over a year! That is so crazy.

What I love to observe is how people are reacting to each other. There is a complete separation going on, and it didn't start with the vaccine.

I remember years ago, I was likely in my 20s, and I was

having a conversation with my mom about people who smoked and drank. I remember asking mom if she thought we were better than them because we didn't do this. More shocking was her answer, "Yes!" "Really?" I countered. "Isn't what they are doing just a choice and says nothing about who they are?" She was silent. She had never thought of that.

The church is where it started for me. When I grew up, I was taught that people who sin are labelled 'less than'. It has always been this way. Ironically, we all sin (their language). Even they who are judging. It's just easier to point a finger when we see their sin versus when we see our own. These thoughts seem so archaic, but it is important to note where some of this judgment started. Who is right and who is wrong has led some major wars and discord with our society for centuries! Just for the record, my mother doesn't think like this anymore, possibly because someone challenged her.

That's also something to note. When you only hang out with people, get lectured by those, or read books by authors with the same point of view as you, you will never grow. This, to me, is also what my church encouraged: only be with those who think like us.

Does it really matter if you are right, and the other person is wrong? Should that even be a thought or a question? Life would be much simpler if we just acknowledged that all decisions are a choice. That's it. It's just a choice without a label.

Let's look at what happened to our First Nations' population with the residential schools. I can't imagine today having a race (Caucasians) determine that another race (Indigenous) needs to conform and be like them. I can't imagine this so-called 'superior' race taking the children of another race (forcefully and without permission from the parents) to teach them how to be their race. Can you teach a race and culture out of a human? The amount of abuse that these little ones and their families endured is just horrific. I have never been more embarrassed to be a white woman in all my life then when I became aware of what really went on.

Why was their race 'wrong'? Why do many people think (and still to this day) that the white man's ways are right? This isn't even a point that should ever be considered, but it has. Converting indigenous peoples to a race that was deemed as right was seen as the right thing to do. It's so absurd that just writing this makes me angry!

Government and religion have been huge instigators into having you think there is a right way and a wrong way. Yet, there are trillions of ways.

The other big player is the health care system and big pharma. They have gained popularity due to their lobbying and wealth. Sick people make the health care system and big pharma loads of money. Why would they want you to be healthy? They would all be out of a job! Have a look down your grocery aisles and just note all the processed foods. Do you think these foods are there to increase your health or keep you from being sick? Why are they approved by our government when regulations are so tight?

Let's get back to where I started with this thought. This 'pandemic' has created sides of thinking that one view is right and one view is wrong. I am talking about people who chose the vaccine and those who did not. I have been asked in my office what church I believe will have the most vaccinated people because that is where this person wanted to go. I calmly said, "I have no idea and you likely never will either. If you are that afraid of non-vaccinated people, you should consider watching church from a screen."

I have also heard of parents telling their new graduate in the house to un-invite all the un-vaccinated friends as we will only have a vaccinated party. These are just two small examples of separation. There are thousands more. This time of my life has shown me how easy it is for us to separate. A person who once was your neighbor or friend is now made your enemy, unless you agree with them, because of their beliefs.

The fear that has been conditioned into us is what creates this separation. For all these examples, religion, government and more recently health care, we have been programmed to believe what is right and what is wrong. Whomever does not agree with their stance is wrong.

Is this really how we want to live? Separate from a society that thinks differently than you? All three of these bodies (religion, government, and health care) represent the people and some under oath of non-discrimination. Yet, they are teaching the very thing that they sometimes preach against. It's very confusing to the human brain if one is not aware enough to catch it. Let's become aware. Let's return to loving all mankind for who s/he is, not for who we want or need them be. This especially applies to family and friends that have been divided by choices. It is also your choice to accept and love without your own conditions.

Thoughts to Ponder:

1. Who in my world have I turned away because they think differently than me?

2. Do I believe that I am always right, and the other person is wrong?

3. What does being right mean to me?

4. What does being wrong mean to me?

5. Who would I love to reconnect with and possibly apologize to?

6. Who do I have accept will never change and let them be?

CHAPTER 6

CHALLENGING OUR BELIEFS

During the writing of this book, I had a big birthday. Yep, I turned 50! Birthdays in the past have never really done much for me. I know some people tell me certain ones are hard or depressing. This one was creeping in, and it felt kind of funny. You see, I don't feel 50 in my mind. In fact, that's staying steady at 35.

About one month before the big bash, my body started acting very weird. My shoulder was so sore I was unable to reach behind my back. My knee was acting like an 80-year-old injury, and my energy levels were sluggish. I just wanted to do nothing. What was going on?

During dinner at my birthday, my dear friend and I started talking about this. She basically said that sometimes at a certain age, people have a belief that they are going downhill and so the body responds. "Oh you want to go downhill and create some suffering? Well, here you go!" Then, the body creates what your subconscious believes. Brilliant, these bodies of ours!

This is much more common than you think. We are so unaware of how our beliefs about aging affect us. Have you ever met up with a friend after a long while, and when you see each other, you can't believe how much that person has aged? Do we believe we are old, so we get old? The opposite is also true. Sometimes you meet up and are surprised they haven't aged at all.

Here's another example of belief. If a doctor said you have about two months to live, would you believe them? If you believe them, would your body respond and die? If your doctor tells you that this is a condition that you will just have to live with, do you believe them, and then live your life with it, not looking for alternative ways or trusting that your body is, in fact, self-regulating and self-healing?

What else do we believe that we really do not have to, but just accept as truth? Think about all the beliefs your family has and may have projected upon you. Here's a few that have been projected on me.

You will always be chubby as you have the Moffet genes.

Your legs will have blue (varicose) veins just like your family.

Your ankles will be bad just like your grandma's.

No, no, no, I don't want any of that!

Think about finances.

You will be poor because your family was poor.

You will struggle because your family struggled.

We never had anything and were happy so you should just be thankful for what you have.

Oh, the projections! Is that what you really want?

I love the saying that it only takes one person to show you what is possible. This means that if you choose another path for your life, you only must see one other person doing it. I am reminded of a business owner in town who has repeatedly told me that when she saw me open a business, she knew she could do it too. When we recognize that people are watching our lives, it holds us accountable to be who we are meant to be by stepping out of our own comfort and doing the 'scary things', like opening a business. You just never know who is watching and needs the push to start their own dream. It is possible that no one showed them or told them what else they can be in this lifetime. Our families cannot teach us everything. I am finding that there are so many younger people stepping beyond their family teachings and wanting even more from life.

A few weeks ago, I was invited to do energy healing at an Indigenous retreat. It was quite an amazing experience. I was in a tent, the ground was my floor, and the lake was just steps away. Trees surrounded us, birds sang, and the people came in, one by one. I was especially curious about a young couple who wanted to see me. They came in separately, yet they shared nearly the same story. They wanted so badly to be loved and accepted by their own family, yet the parents did not seem emotionally capable of giving the love that these young people needed. We talked about that and how they knew a different love was out there, but they likely were looking in the wrong place for it.

This couple desperately wanted to show their kids a new life and new love. They were breaking the family patterns and reaching for something more. I felt so honored that they shared their story with me. I know they were relieved to hear they did not have to be their parents and they have everything within them to create something more for their kids.

I almost think we feel we are betraying our family when we do not adopt their beliefs. This can be about anything. Where does it say that we must believe everything that our family does? When we think and do this, we stay stuck in our family lines, and we do not progress in our evolution.

Challenge your beliefs. Hang out with people who think differently than you. If you want something in life (health, finance, great relationships, etc.) spend time with people who have that. What you see in others, you have in yourself!

Thoughts to Ponder:

1. What do I believe about my health?
2. What do I believe about my age?
3. Where in my life do I challenge my family's beliefs?
4. Who is living a life that I desire?

CHAPTER 7

LEARNING FROM LITTLE TRAUMAS

I saw a meme on social media where a person is basically telling us that they are done with self-improvement and just going to 'settle and live'. I kind of laughed at it as I have felt this so many times, yet my soul knew I would only ever take breaks and never stop trying to improve my life. In fact, one day as I was contemplating retirement, my soul was the one to have a good laugh and said, "You didn't come back to this planet to retire."

Oh, there is so much here to unpack.

Self-improvement is a funny thing. No one ever wants someone else to tell them when and how to improve. When we are ready, we may hire a coach or a therapist, or do some digging on our own, but no one wants someone to tell them they need to improve, and how to do it.

Every day in my practice, people pay me to help them improve. It may be as simple as helping their muscles feel better with massage or as complex as helping them with a stuck emotion that is bringing up trauma from their childhood. People ask me for it; they pay me for it. They are ready for it. Then, they feel so good that they want their partner to experience it too. They sometimes buy a gift certificate for them. This is where things go all wrong.

No one wants help unless they ask for it. I can't tell you how many times the partner doesn't come in and the client ends up using it themself, or worse, the partner no-shows me and the gift is used as payment. This has shown me that we cannot force improvement upon others. They must choose it on their own.

I don't really understand why anyone would just want to be done with improving their life. I don't really understand why people stop learning or exploring things that interest them. There are so many things to explore and yet there are many people disconnected and living without purpose. Why not learn something new or set a new goal or start a business?

My husband just quoted a recent study that had to do with men and depression saying that majority of men diagnosed with depression don't have hobbies. This is such an important piece of life. Hobbies provide joy. Joy vibrates super high. Hobbies give us a little purpose and meaning. It reminded me of all the people who retire and are so bored that they find a part time job.

I started a side business awhile back. I have done this from time to time, but this was something that really grabbed my attention. I wasn't looking to add anything to what I currently do. It just fell in my lap, and I knew I needed to be involved. This business included learning about frequency tools and how to use them to help heal the body.

As I started using this terahertz frequency on my body, I noticed that my body was holding on to cellular memory. Only now was it showing me the emotions that I held from past injuries. When I looked at these emotions, I was able to bring my awareness to the past and heal. How? It's simple really. All our little traumas are held in the body until we release them. The body is brilliant in how it shows us what needs to be looked at. If you or someone you love has a lot of body pain or their body holds conditions or disease, they likely have not looked at nor processed their traumas, emotions or loss.

Here is one old memory that I discovered and how I processed it. When I was 15, I went downhill skiing with friends. I never had a lesson, just winged it. We didn't have mountains where I lived; it was a glorified large hill. On this particular ski adventure, I fell so hard that I couldn't walk the next day. My entire thigh was bruised. It hurt. It healed, but not completely. I still have remnants of a bruise on that leg. As I was using this frequency tool, the memory of that accident showed up. I hadn't thought about this memory in years. I started to explore my feelings around the fall. This is how you can start to heal the trauma. You must take a look.

I remember falling and then hearing laughing from people on the ski lift above me. I don't remember anyone asking if I was okay or comforting me. I'm sure someone did, but I don't remember who was there. The real trauma was being laughed at, even though I was in physical pain. I kind of had a boyfriend at the time. He was there, but I don't remember him even asking if I was okay. I don't recall him there at all. I remember going home and telling my family about the fall. I don't remember any care at home or special attention. I did not go to the doctor to get checked out. It really seemed like no one cared that I was in pain. Almost as though I was invisible or tough, I decided I didn't need codling. I was 15. I was a big girl.

I am 50 now. My 50-year-old self held my 15-year-old self in my mind's eye, and we had a conversation.

50-year-old self: That was quite the fall. How are you feeling?

15-year-old self: Ignored. Invisible, as if I don't matter, or no one has time to check in on me.

50-year-old self: I'm here. You matter. Ask your body what it needs. Let me help you put up your leg and rest. I'll get some ice.

15-year-old self: Okay, thanks.

50-year-old self: Tell me what happened and are you hurt anywhere else? Would you like to see a doctor?

15-year-old self: My whole body hurts, but my heart hurts even more as it felt like no one cared. This was probably the most damage I have ever done to my body, and I was laughed at and treated like it didn't matter.

50-year-old self: It does matter. You matter. I'm glad it wasn't anything worse. Sometimes people don't know how to be or how to respond to traumas like this. They think that if things are not broken, then you can just suck it up and wait to heal. What really matters is how you process all these feelings. It also matters that you realize how people respond is a 'them' thing. It really has nothing to do with you. You may want something completely different, but they are not conscious enough to be able to give that to you. You must learn to process this pain in your own way and give yourself what you need. It sucks when you are young and cannot understand this, but when you are older, you will.

15-year-old self: I feel better already.

If you end up having a memory like this, hold each other until there is no pain and no remnants of what you 'wished' had happened before your older version showed up. It is that easy to rewrite the cellular memory, so that the body has a chance to continue to heal and remove the last remnants of trauma.

It surprises me how someone would not want to delete the entire pain from their body, cells, and being. Never stop learning. There is so much that we can explore inside and outside of our bodies. While we have these bodies, we may as well learn all we can and evolve as deeply as we can so that we can leave the planet a better place.

Will I ever retire? Likely not, as there are too many things to learn and to share from what I learn. This is my greatest assignment while I am human. This assignment never ends until the final breath and even then, it may carry on.

Thought to Ponder:

1. What would you like to learn while you are here and human?

2. Do you need a hobby?

3. Have you ever explored your own little traumas? Maybe it's time to take a look and have conversations with yourself?

CHAPTER 8

FEMININE POWER

I never knew my dad desired to have a boy until much later in life. We were casually driving home from the lake, and I asked him if he had any regrets in life. He said he wished he had a boy to do things with.

There is just my sister and me. Likely, before I was born, there were high hopes that I was a boy. My 'boy name' was picked out already: 'Marno'. Thank God I was a girl, as I'm not too sure about that name! Marno was my uncle who passed away very young after being run over. I think he had 5 years on the planet.

When my sister and I were young, my grandpa would sing to us and record it. I distinctly remember one time purposely trying to sound like a boy. When Jodi (my sister) played it back for me years later, she was wondering who the boy was. Yeah, that's me. She didn't believe it to be true. It was 40 years later, and the memories came flooding back. (These random snippets of my life that I'm sharing will have a purpose here; just stay with me.)

I have also written about an old story in my first book about walking home from kindergarten (yes, different times in the '70s when kids walked home from school by themselves) and being sat on by a fat kid. My friends and sister watched, not realizing it was four against one. But we were girls, and he was a boy. What could we do?

It occurred to me very recently that I have always wanted to be a boy/man. I did not accept this gender 100%. I saw how the male species was favored, and more wanted. I grew my body large to protect me from the kindergarten kids. I lowered my voice to sound like a boy. I was always strong, still am. Why did I not want to be a girl? I still struggle with the color pink, and sometimes force myself to buy and wear it. What is going on here?

It wasn't until very recently that this was brought to my attention through Bill McKenna (founder of Cognomovement). He spoke about how he was working with a client, and she had extreme menstrual pain which took her out for a week at a time each month. This client was now in her forties and he was astonished with how much life she spent in pain, in a fetal position on the couch until it passed.

I related to this pain as each month, for just a day, maybe two, my body hurts and I am not myself. Advil is my friend and I usually pop a couple to keep going. Even as a teen this was the case, and it was much worse then, where I experienced near black outs.

Bill suggested embracing the feminine goddess within to balance the pain of menstruating and possibly menopause. "Embrace the feminine goddess". Okay, how the heck do we do that?

Any time you deny a part of yourself you have a missing piece, just floating around waiting to be discovered. This is the same as I mentioned in the earlier chapters of not wanting to be here and calling the missing pieces of our life back. Is it possible that I didn't want to be this gender because of inequality from our history? Even in my lifetime, I have seen this inequality, as though the man is greater than the woman.

For me, there is no better place to observe this than through our history, and particularly the church. I have not been a part of a church in a few decades now so I'm sure I'd find some differences today. When I used to go to church (and sometimes up to 5 times a week when I was young), women were not allowed to lead, speak, or show any type of opinion really. They weren't allowed to be on the church board to have any decision-making power. Women were silent, just like in the home.

Christians are still taught that the man is the leader of the home. There is no equality. The man has the final say – that's what the bible (written and interpreted by men) says.[1]

Whoa, whoa, whoa! So you're telling me that I am to submit to a man and that I am a secondary species on the planet? I am less than a man? Well, no wonder I wanted to be a man! I wanted to be seen, accepted, heard, and loved.

In about 2017ish, we were having a family dinner and my grandpa (who was in his 90s at that time) said something along the lines of Grandma having to obey him, because he is the head of the house. I started laughing. "Grandpa, do you really think of Grandma as less than you? I thought you were partners?" I was the only one engaged in this conversation, because the rest of my family has the same belief as my grandpa. My grandpa was a bit taken back (because he is a thinker and no one has ever challenged this thought… because when you hang around people who think the same as you, nothing ever gets challenged).

We never brought this up again, but here is where my conditioning started in this lifetime. I was born into this way of thinking. After my first marriage and likely during it, I never thought of one of us as greater than. We were partners. We were equals. My family may argue back with "Well, who has the final say?" We both do and sometimes

---

1 Corinthians 11:13 "But I want you to realize that the head of every man is Christ, and the head of the woman is man"

we agree to disagree and that's okay!

Women in our history and in different cultures have been treated like a mistake, or sex objects, trained to look good, and be eye candy for the male species. Women have been seen as those who can look after the kids and home so that the men can go out and do whatever they want with their careers and recreation.

Our generation right now are the change makers. I am so delighted when I hear about men who cook, clean, help raise the kids, and treat their partner with respect. They allow her to chase her dreams and build a life together. I think about some of the older generations that I know where the women were severely suppressed.

I had a great aunt who only started living in her 90s because her husband was so controlling and suspicious of what she did. He suppressed her life until his death. Only then did she start living freely. When I got divorced, she told me I was lucky. I had never heard that from anyone, and after exploring this issue a bit, I understood what she really meant. She was unable to live. On a side note here, I hope you don't ever wait until you are in your 90s to live!

Calling back this part of you that you have hidden is reclaiming your identity. This is all a part of the second chakra located just above the pubic bone. This chakra is connected to our reproductive organs and hormones. This part of us may have been in pain, suffering for our gender. When we step into our power of being a woman, just acknowledging this, we activate the energy needed to free the stuck frustration it has caused in our lifetime. There are some mind-body ways to uncover more of this, as it is individualized in what you have experienced in your lifetime, just as it has been for me. If you are suffering with menstrual or menopausal difficulties, you may be unbalanced energetically in this area.

I will imagine a world where the women stand in their power. Where they hold their head high and celebrate the feminine goddess within. It is safe to be a woman. It is time to be an equal and step fully into ourselves.

I have wondered why there are so many female alternative health practitioners right now. It's very lopsided when going to classes, workshops, and retreats. The men are starting to show up, and likely these brave souls have embraced their own feminine power as we have both masculine and feminine within us. It is obvious, too, how men have been suppressed to express their feminine side. It is safe to express and embrace all sides of us. We are partners on the planet. We are equals and offer our uniqueness as opposite genders.

Thoughts to Ponder:

1. Have you ever been told you were less than because of your gender?

2. Have you noticed any suppressed females in your family lines?

3. For the women reading this, do you have menstrual or menopausal symptoms?

4. Are you ready to step into your power and claim your right to exist as a female or male?

CHAPTER 9

THE ENERGY OF SAFE

Silence is all around me. This old house is cracking in the cold. I am tired of the winter and desire warmth, light, and more excitement. We stay in our homes, sheltered from the elements. We rarely play outside as an adult in these frigid northern Canadian conditions.

I do love my home. I enjoy 'coming home.' I say prayers of thanks for what it provides. Sometimes that is as simple as the sheets on my bed and a roof over my head. I feel extremely fortunate. We do not live in lavishness, but we are very comfortable. Our needs are met and more.

The home is created for a person to feel safe, at least for most people. There are some, of course, for whom this is not a true statement. Feeling safe has been key for these last few years of living in a world that seems to be in chaos. Do you feel safe in your home?

Safety is the sense of calm. It's the feeling of contentment. It's knowing that you fit in and are welcome no matter what you have done or have been through.

I remember when I was camping as a kid, my friends and I went fishing in a creek. We rode our bikes and carried our rods that were all ready to catch some little perch fish. On our way there, I wiped out on my bike and got the fishhook stuck in my upper chest. It didn't really hurt, but I was scraped up and bleeding. My friends rode with me all the way back to our campsite to find my mom. I remember the feeling as though it were yesterday. As soon as I saw her, I started to cry. I even remember asking my little self, why am I crying now? I hadn't been crying for the last 20 minutes since falling. I believe it was the feeling of safety. I am safe. I made it to my mom. I can be myself. I was actually really scared, but now, all is well.

For those of us who are still fortunate to have our moms, there was a recent study I heard about where if you hear your mom's voice, your cortisol levels decrease giving you a feeling of less stress. If you get a text from your mom, it's not the same. There is something in the voice that calms the child.

This is what our home environment should be for all of us.

The people in our environment should be calm, supportive and filled with love no matter what we have been through that day. It should be our place where we say "Ahhhhh, I'm home!"

I know some of you reading this are wishing that 'so and so' in your house would agree with you and make things easier for you to come home to. Well, 'so and so' is responsible for themself. You are responsible for you! This is where you always start when you desire something different, with yourself. Maybe it's time to create a space in your home that gives you this feeling, a place that is just for you.

Look around your space, indoors and out. Does it support your safe feeling? Is it comforting and soothing? Does it fill you with joy and contentment? What can you change to make it that way? Is it filled with your favorite things or cluttered with things that just overwhelm you? Clean it up. Honor your space. It will give back to you in greater ways.

Obvious to me, and likely to you too, is if you do not feel safe, you need to get out. If your physical and mental/emotional well-being is being harmed, it is time for you to leave. This will likely be the hardest decision in your life, but you are worthy of feeling safe, content, and loved each time you come home to your space.

You can overcome the fear of leaving an unsupportive space by looking to the people who have done it before you (and there have been many). If 'so and so' can do it, you can too. This is my mantra in life when I'm scared. Ask for courage and be brave. The people who have done this before you believed they were worthy of something greater and so are you! There is no difference between you and them.

If you are the one creating the chaos for your family and not allowing them to feel safe, it's time to ask yourself, "How's that working for me?" Are you ready to try something completely different? Where in your own life has your own security been breached? Do you need help to explore those instances so that you can be free to move on?

The energy of safety is completely grounding and powerful. Imagine something in your life where you go to check it and you say, "Now, that's secure." This should be us! All of us. When you are safe, you feel secure. When you feel secure, you have enough power within you to choose whatever you want to do with your life at any moment. Even if you make a choice that doesn't work out so well, you can choose again. You will have a soft place to land, because your home life is safe.

Create that for yourself. The energy of safety is like none other.

Thoughts to Ponder:

1. Do I feel safe in my home?

2. Am I causing my family to feel safe or unsafe?

3. What can I do to create a safer environment for myself and my family?

PART 2

BITS IN BETWEEN

Nobody realizes that some people expend tremendous energy merely to be normal.

- Albert Camus

CHAPTER 10

THE ENERGY OF WEATHER

It amazes me how some cultures never talk about the weather. I should live there. Where I live (northern Saskatchewan, Canada), the weather is a daily topic. It is small talk. When you have nothing else to say you talk about the weather and then move on to how the crops are doing or are going to do. Both conversations bore me to the core, but it's unavoidable in this town.

Last night our little 1950s house was cracking. We knew the cold snap was coming. The cracks make me think the house is going to fall down. The cracks disturb my cats and make them jump. It went to minus 35 Celsius overnight.

This is how we plan for a deep freeze. We make sure the cars are plugged in. We turn up the furnace. We try not to plan anything for the morning as it will be quite hard to get out of bed and outside. If we do have to leave the house, we warm up the car for about 20 minutes and still drive on what seems like square tires. We try not to plan out of town trips on these days, because people have literally frozen to death having highway troubles. Most people have emergency kits in their vehicles.

As I woke up, it was so quiet. Likely some school buses didn't run. I'm sure many cars didn't start. The day care next door had zero screaming kids this morning (some days it's unbearable). It was very peaceful. That's the only upside. It settles us down.

In this community, the weather changes at least 70 degrees Celsius over the year and usually much more. Therefore, people talk about it. It's extreme, and it plays on our moods, our energy.

If we look to nature in how it just 'is' through all the extremes, maybe we would be able to mimic the way to be as we wake up to the highs and lows. All things slow down in the cold. In the winter, birds go south to find warmer weather, as do many of our seniors and retirees. Animals hibernate. Humans should do that a little more too, but they push themselves to do as much as they can, and then wonder why they get sick. We are working against nature when we push.

The energy of our winter is slower, more reflective. We work on projects. We stay cozy and warm. We play in the snow a bit, but we spend more time indoors as the darkness takes over. It is a time to go within, to work on ourselves and all the things we neglect when summer comes.

As the weather warms, we are outside a lot more. Our energy is quicker, our schedules are fuller. We are more active; our spirits are brighter usually. The sun plays a part, and the vitamin D is huge for our bodies to function with more life. The energy of summer is happier. People are a bit more pleasant and social. It's different.

From my experience of living in this climate (for 35+ years), people dread the winter and live for the summer. As I'm writing this, I'm realizing it's likely because we are not moving with the energy of the seasons. It's possible, as noted previously, that we push our entire being into activity, when all it wants to do is hibernate, slow down and rest. Some people reading this might think that I am promoting being a hermit. It's not that at all.

Even though weather is something that most people around here find easy to talk about, it also produces something that's harder to talk about. When our energy changes because of the weather changes, a lot of people find it hard to cope mentally.

My hardest month of the year is usually November. I have started talking a lot more about this. People see my life and think it's all roses, but this is the month I really struggle.

Yes, I may put on the happy face, but secretly I cannot wait to crawl back into bed after a day out and about.

I do not want to be controlled by the weather. I don't want it to have any power over my mentality. Since I am aware that it does this, each year I have been preparing better for it. I usually get away in November. Even if it's somewhere close to home. This past year I worked on my nutrition and moving my body more. I have complete awareness each day of how I feel.

The preparation this year helped a lot. There is so much we can do, but we don't do it. That could be a theme for many people. If you want change, you must be the change. No one is going to do it for you.

Is there a possibility to enjoy all the weather, not just one season? You can decide. I am still amused that talking about the weather daily is one of the strangest things my community does!

Thoughts to Ponder:

1. What are your thoughts on the seasons. Do you like one more than the other?

2. Is there a month that is more difficult for you mentally during the year?

3. What can you do to change that?

CHAPTER 11

TAKING ON OTHER'S ENERGY

(Part 1)

This is such a huge topic. Nearly every time I teach an energy class or a reiki class, this comes up. I love how people are becoming more and more familiar that taking on another person's energy is possible. It is possible to take on another's energy and even feel the physical symptoms that they are experiencing.

How may you ask? Well, you first must acknowledge that you are energy. Then you need to explore the energy field and how far from your body it extends. In my first book, I wrote about a demonstration that I do with homemade witching wands. They are programmed to find energy fields. These are simple wands made of wire coat hangers and pen holders. You can invest in some pricier ones coming out of India called 'Universal Aura Scanners', which evolve from age old dowsing modalities. I have given my own set a job, which is to find energy fields. They flare out when they hit an energy field. It's still fun to play with and watch them do what they are told.

From my experimenting, most people's energy fields are about an arm's length all around their body. Some may even say that our body is inside of us. This field around our body is also us. The denser complex physical form is right in the middle. This body is how we experience life. Possibly, when we die, we just ditch the body, and the energy form is still there. That may be why we feel a loved one's presence. Without this body, we can travel and move in greater ways than say on an airplane. This is my belief. You do not have to adopt it, but if it resonates with you, there may be some truth for you to explore.

When we are in a crowd, just think about that arm's length and how many people are in your field and how many fields you are also in. This can apply to concerts, an airplane, or a mall or anywhere there are crowds. You can reach out and touch people.

The other day my husband and I were travelling on a plane and when we landed, the airport was super crowded. Kids were crying. We were shoulder to shoulder at times with fellow travellers. It made us question why we chose to travel on a holiday weekend. We both started getting a little cranky. I said to Craig, "Don't ask me how this works or how it's done, but just command your energy field to contract!" I'm sure he rolled his eyes, but just him listening to that statement was enough to produce the 'change of possibility'. I can't tell you how many times we have travelled, and we were so grumpy by the time we reached the hotel. When we checked in, we ended up getting the room overlooking the air conditioning units or right by the elevators or some other less than delightful room. What would be possible if we arrived and had great energy exuding from our field? Would we get a free upgrade?

Line ups for the rental car were slow and when we finally got in the car, it was like a breath of fresh air. We made it through the crowds of grumpy, tired, unpleasant travellers. On we went to our resort destination, turned some music on, commented on the scenery and eventually arrived at our hotel. It was pleasant. The check in was pleasant. The room was even more pleasant. What just happened here? Did we create the ability to enjoy the day of travel? Did we just command our energy to contract, so that we could not pick up other's energy as easily?

When you contract your energy field, it comes right close to your skin. You cannot feel people's stuff and they cannot feel yours. It's just you, living in your own bubble. I desire a life that is all this, just living in our own energy and not affected by others' points of view or energy.

Being affected by others is only a problem when the

vibration is low.

Think now about an emotionally moving concert. You may even have a tear in your eye as you share this moment with tens of thousands of people. You are also feeling this good vibration and likely wouldn't want it to shut off or contract your energy from it. Another example is being in a home with your loved ones. Your energy field in its full expansion as it is safe and welcomed. These are the people you love the most on the planet.

So how do you decide when to expand and when not to?

To answer this, we need to go back to remembering what 'good' in the body feels like and what 'not so good/scattered/chaotic/anxious/fearful' feels like. If we are in tune with our bodies, this is quite easy. Then we make the decision.

Right now, just stop what you're reading and ask yourself how you are feeling? Ask your body how it's feeling and what it needs to feel as good as it can. Notice I don't ask for high vibration as what is high for one may not be high for another. What is your normal state of feeling good? What does it feel like inside yourself to say "Yes, this is me. I feel good."

Once you have that baseline, then it is very easy to know when you are off or even when you are being influenced by outside energy. When you identify that you are off, only then can you make the decisions to do something about it. You may decide to contract or expand or give the body, mind, spirit what it needs to re-calibrate. This one, tiny little shift in your awareness has potential for you to be playing a whole new game in a whole new ballpark. Once you start playing with this, keep the awareness and conversation with yourself going forever.

We should always operate on our own energy, but sometimes we are not vibrating at a healthy resonance ourselves, and so we will attract more of that same vibration. Like attracts like. If you want to have a shitty day and complain about it, you will find other people who like to do the same. If you want to dream and plan and give gratitude for what is presented in your life, you will find those people who do the same, and more opportunity to express yourself with these attributes. Your vibration will attract the vibration that you most hang out in.

Many times, when we are doing something we love, or hanging out with our favorite people on the planet, or just surrounded by what brings us joy, our fields will expand very large. This is why it's so fun to hang out with certain people. Their energy fields are so inviting. We always get to decide how we want to present to the world. Do you want to be a prickly field or an inviting one? This would be a great time to re-evaluate what you desire and who you are hanging out with.

Thoughts to Ponder:

1. What does 'normal energy' feel like to you in your

body?

2. Right now, is your energy low, normal, or high?
3. What are three things you can do to raise or lower your vibrations?

CHAPTER 12

TAKING ON OTHER'S ENERGY

(Part 2)

This is such a loaded topic it deserves two chapters.

Now that you have identified that there is some funky energy going on in your body and you are not sure if it is even yours, how do you test it to know for sure, and what can you do about it?

If you have identified what feeling 'normal' is for you, you are halfway there. It's easy to know that it's not yours if you are doing great one moment and then if someone walks in the room, whom you may not even know, and your energy internally shifts. Something feels weird (different than 'normal for you') and there is no reason for your energy to have changed other than this person coming into the room.

Could it be that you are feeling their energy?

Hell, yes!

Could that energy be set at a different frequency than yours? You bet. You may be such a sensitive soul that you start to feel it in your body. Maybe you feel their knee pain or headache or their emotions. This happens, and no, you are not crazy; you are just energy.

Think of it without the body. If two energy fields collided, would one affect the other? We feel so much of what is going on, but we second guess it all because of our humanness. Just take the humanness out of it.

The first question to ask is "Is this mine?"

Okay, I know what you're saying "How do I hear the answer?" A lot of people are not going to hear it, but they may feel it or have a sense of knowing the answer. So don't wait for that audible Jesus moment of someone talking in your ear. It likely won't happen. This is where using your intuition comes in. You will know. The more you play with this the easier it becomes. You likely remember me talking about the clairs. Your most dominant ones will give you the answer.

If the answer is "NO, this is not my energy", ask it to be

returned to whom it belongs to. If this energy goes away immediately and you return to your 'normal for you' state, then it wasn't yours. It was called out and you were strong enough and aware enough to tell it to bugger off. Well done! All you need to do is just be aware that they (and you may not even know who 'they' is) have funky energy. You don't have to analyze it or judge where it came from or anything really; it just is.

Another way is to stand in the power of your 8th Chakra (see Chapter 17 for info on the 8th chakra) and ask that all energy and programming from this lifetime and all other lifetimes that does not serve your highest good to leave your energy field now. When you say this, you may feel tired or even feel a shift. It is possible that you will feel nothing. Something will be shown to you in the form of another vibration. Possibly you will have the awareness to clear the energy to help yourself, and even humanity, progress to higher vibrations.

It is becoming increasingly clear that we have been programmed all our life. Some of it is out of unconscious intent, such as family trying to love by control. Likely some is with conscious content, such as the daily news being owned by the powers that be, telling you what they want you to hear and not really the news that is happening in the world that may concern you. This happens in movies or institutions too. They are brilliant and have played a role in shaping your thinking and, one could say, your energy. Have you ever wondered why they call it a television program?

Here's another crazy thought. What if some of the thinking you have and even the actions you do are from thoughts and programming from other lifetimes? Do we carry that with us when we reincarnate? I guess if you don't believe in reincarnation, you will be skipping this part.

Recently I launched an online coaching program. I know the material inside and out and I put it out there to the world to be seen, and advertised for people to sign up. As soon as I did that, thoughts and negative conversations started flooding my head. "You're not good enough to teach anything; everyone knows this material." "No one's going to participate in this." "No one can afford the luxury of taking this self-development course." And on and on it went.

Whoa, what is all this? Where did it come from? These are not thoughts I think every day or about myself. How did they just suddenly appear in my consciousness out of nowhere? Were they already there, and I just had to do something to trigger them to come to the surface? And, are they even mine?

What do you do with these thoughts? I don't want them in my space! Also, no one talks about how to get rid of these energetically. Just google "how to get rid of negative thoughts." The answers will not help people if they don't deal with the energy behind them. They will just keep coming up.

What if these thoughts are coming up so that we can clear them for our own inner growth? We also must consider we might be clearing this energy from our ancestors and the collective consciousness. "What the heck are you talking about, Cari?" See I really can hear your voice!

I'm talking about the possibility that our family had these thoughts and then never acted on the things that scared them, because they chose comfort and survival over dreams and ambitions. I'm also talking about how we are part of it all, and that includes the collective of all that is, every damn person who has had a thought. We are influenced by the collective. I'm sure I don't have to remind you of Covid. The fear there was very collective. We stayed in our homes scared to hug one another.

What if it's time for humanity to step up? What if we are being called to something greater? These lower vibrational thoughts are possibly coming up for us to be aware of and then to examine them and clear them.

Clearing them is done exactly as I described above. Stand in your power and tell them to leave. This is with everything. You don't have to go into this long exhaustive ritual of putting on music, lighting candles, finding a guru and 'seancing' them out. You are the powerful magical being and can do exactly this. Become aware of what it is and tell it to go! Just like you would a trespasser. This is the same. If you feel you need help, like how we sometimes need the police, then ask an energy worker to assist you in moving through some lower vibrations in and around your body. We give so much power to other teachers or methods when really, it's YOU who is the powerful one. YOU have just forgotten.

Here are some practical ways to release energy from the body.

1. Go outside, walk barefoot, if possible, and breathe deep.

2. Take a shower or bath or jump into a body of water.

3. Move your body, dance, exercise, run, walk.

4. Express what you are feeling out loud or on paper or in your mind.

5. Get some energy work done e.g. Reiki, or better yet, go for regular appointments to maintain your well-being.

Thoughts to Ponder:

What comes up when you declare:

1. I AM POWERFUL.

2. I AM MAGICAL.

3. I AM FEARLESS.

CHAPTER 13

THE ENERGY OF PRIDE

I remember a fight my husband and I had. Somehow, we got arguing about our office and I must have said something to which he replied, "You're pretty proud of that aren't you!" Now, I could have retracted my statement (and I can't recall what it was even), but instead I replied, "Yes, I am proud of creating Wholelife Wellness from nothing." This is the brick-and-mortar company I started back in 2008.

Why did I have the thought of denying my pride? I believe it's because this is what we are taught. *You shouldn't be this way. You shouldn't put it out there that you've accomplished something great and wave it with a sense of achievement. How big is your ego anyway?*

Are you relating to this? If we cannot celebrate and be proud of what we've accomplished, then why the heck do we do these hard things!!!

My dear friend was telling me she was nearly mortgage free. She's in her thirties, on her own, living in a city. Her house was nearly paid for. I asked her how she is going to celebrate. "What a great idea!" she replied.

I'm wondering how many people celebrate this accomplishment. It's a huge deal when the bank no longer owns one of your greatest assets. She concluded that she may throw a party!

Some of these things are massive and some of these things that deserve a celebration are just tiny. Still, why not enjoy and observe your accomplishments? Gosh, we celebrate our birthdays and really, what have we done? We just lived another year, without even trying that hard. When you pay off your mortgage or start a business or write a book or get a good grade on an exam, why not take that time to celebrate!?

I was laying on a massage table a few months back and my shoulder was getting worked on. Being a massage therapist myself, I feel like I've overused it to a point where it's not functioning as it should. I started thinking about someone in my life who abuses the 'pride' word and uses it as a power trip. She always wants the credit for everything that happens even when she is the one who causes the stressors that get resolved. Pride can be skewed to come out as arrogance. Arrogance is exaggerating one's own worth or importance often in an overbearing manner. They show a sense of superiority. This is also a representation of unbalanced energy in the body.

Pride for celebration and pride of arrogance are completely different. Likely no one has ever taught us the difference, and so they all clump together in the same low vibratory category.

When I noticed I was thinking about pride while getting work done on my shoulder, I started to ask my body if this is what it is holding on to – the inability to be proud of all I accomplished so far in my career and life. I had a resounding YES from my body, followed by a deep breath. Then it made me want to start to cry a sweet emotional release to what I was holding.

This is just a small piece of information that disconnects us from the true magical potent being that we are. We possibly don't believe that we are worth celebrating and our bodies will hold on to that until we are ready to acknowledge it!

As I continued to work it out and recognized the connection, I was also aware of my body clearing energy for the collective. The commanding statements I used (and am still using) are, "Everywhere I have been taught that pride is wrong and evil, I stand in my power and return that to where it started, never to return to my body or energy field again! Everywhere it runs in my DNA and ancestral lines, I transmute it to love. I release it from my body, energy field, and collective consciousness."

Until more of this gets cleared on our planet, we may be stuck in not being able to celebrate our greatness. You may find that when you want to celebrate 'you', others will think you are being egotistical, and you will hide your brilliance from the rest of the world. This is such a sad state. We all have so much to share and joy to reflect, yet sometimes no one to share it with.

I made a Facebook post recently that I went back to edit because to the common person it would sound 'all about me' and very arrogant. In my post I put added this statement '(said in my most non-arrogant way)' and yet I still felt like I had to delete the entire post. I don't feel like I'm an egocentric person, yet I am sensitive to others and how they perceive me. I should say, "I don't give a shit" but I do. We all do, and yada yada, don't tell me you don't, because I know deep down you do, and that you are affected by rude, cruel, unconscious people.

If we all became a society where we celebrated our brilliance, well then likely I would have been able to keep the post up with good conscience. I can hear my coach now, "Ahh Cari, step into your power and celebrate all of you." Oh, I'm trying and I'm navigating this tricky public presence, because my energy is not the same as majority.

I do believe that the things I struggle with are what the world and my circle are possibly trying to get towards and sometimes we need pioneers to show us the way. We need people to show us how to celebrate ourselves more than just on our birthdays!

Thoughts to Ponder:

1. What have you done in your life that you are super proud of? Think of at least 10 things.

2. Have you celebrated your accomplishments? How will you celebrate your next big goal?

3. How can you celebrate weekly, maybe daily, all that you are?

CHAPTER 14

THE ENERGY OF CONTROL

Control is another subject that has come up in my massage practice. When the theme keeps occurring, I always perk up to pay attention, as my energy is always attracting the same energy. This means that this is a message for me as much as my client.

My first client of the week came in suffering with low back pain. She knew she overdid it at the gym. She blamed her dead lifts and when I touched her low back, it had another story for her. It told me the story of wanting to be in control and not trusting the flow of life. I asked her back (yes, you likely know by now I'm that crazy and talk to bodies) what it meant by not trusting the flow? Her body replied, "She doesn't trust me when I say it's too much".

The body holds such wisdom and never lies. It gives us messages all throughout the day. Some are easy to hear like "I'm hungry." Some are very tricky as in this case "That's too much."

I relayed these messages and the client laughed in agreement. I asked her when the last time was that she felt she was in the flow. When was the last time she listened to spirit and her body and took the action it was asking for? She said she is generally very in tune with her body, but she didn't trust its message. "Let's explore trust, then", I said. "Where and when in your life has trust been misunderstood? What or who allowed you not to trust?" Deep thoughts for a massage.

I sent her on her way to think about what we discussed and to ask more questions from her body. There is so much to explore if we only will listen.

In walks the next client. She was experiencing low back pain. She was struggling with her son's behaviour. I put my hands on her back, and it started telling me the same story. (What the heck!?) This mom wanted to control the situation. She was unable to allow the flow to unravel with her son. She was unable to allow him to make mistakes. She was unable to allow him to be him and find his own way and to be his own person without interfering.

Why is this so hard? Why do we want people to do life the

way we do it? Why do we think our way is the only way? There are so many ways to do things and, news flash, your way isn't the only way! The thoughts you have are not the way everyone thinks. Get over yourself and allow the flow of other ways to permeate around you. You may even learn something!

Off this client goes into the world after our session and I can only hope that she can release the parental reins a little. Her son would bond with her more if she did, I'm sure of it.

My next client of the day was a phone consult, and it revealed with the same message. With the theme repeating all day, I knew that these messages were for me as well.

This client was struggling with her daughter's choices, so much so that it was causing her anxiety. This should be an easy coaching call, as I have just practiced this message with my last two clients.

When is the last time you felt a flow, an ease or calmness in your life? What does that even mean and look like? Imagine someone close to you is choosing something that you think is wrong. Instead of telling them they are wrong and to do it this way, just allow them to have that experience. Sometimes our experiences are met with consequences, and just allow them to have those as well. Of course, if you sense their life is in danger, step in. Or, if someone will be harmed, step in. Otherwise, just allow them to be them and to make their own decisions.

At the time this was all going on around me, I was in a push pull relationship with the world. I too was not allowing the flow to happen all around me. It was during the pandemic. I found myself remembering trauma as a child and was triggered by being controlled and not being able to do what I deemed was right or wanted to do. Covid also brought up not being able to do what we wanted when we wanted and many of us felt controlled and stuck. We were not in the flow of life.

When I recognized that these people were coming to me to show me this lesson, I had a major shift and memory surfaced of what it is like to be in the flow. This 'flow' is easy, fun, joyful, and full of love, optimism, and happiness. It's where I want to be as much as I can. I want to trust my spirit and my body with the messages that come up. Just imagine for a moment how freeing this flow will feel in your life when you release the need to control all things or people around you.

Thoughts to Ponder:

1. Does your body have a message for you? Ask it!

2. Have you noticed a repeat of messages or conversations in your own life? Is the message possibly for you?

3. What does the flow mean for you in your life?

4. Is there something you need to release your grip of control from?

CHAPTER 15

CONNECTIONS AND CORDS

It was a beautiful fall day, and I had a lady on my table requesting 30 minutes of Reiki. I knew that she had witnessed a horrific death just months prior. We didn't even go into it, because truthfully the story is just the story. When we talk about it all the time and with people constantly, it becomes part of our identity. I'm not sure you want that. The story isn't you; it's what has happened to and around you. In saying this, our story is useful to tell a trusted soul to express the energy out of our body. In this case, we just focused on the energy of what was in and around her body.

With Reiki, the traditional hand placements are all over the chakras. A practitioner will feel or sense changes in that area if the energy centre (chakra) is unbalanced in any way. My hands were drawn to her heart. It was thick and heavy. I knew it needed more time and so I stayed there.

Reiki isn't me healing a person. Reiki is tapping into the source energy that some call God, Universe, Creator, etc. and asking for help. I then allow that help to flow through me to give the person whatever it is that they are needing. Don't worry if you pray to God and the Reiki practitioner prays to Creator. The energy of the prayer is the same and will find the frequency you connect to. Most energy practitioners will deem it all the same and respect your beliefs. Your ego must get out of the way and not judge or be fearful of the method. They are not tapping into an evil source, that's for sure, because there is no healing there.

As my hands were sitting at this woman's heart centre, I had a completely random memory of my childhood. My parents had just sold their house and my mom had kept a box of stuff that was mine from childhood. I went through every single paper and threw out 99% of it. In one yearbook I had written nasty things about a few of the people. It embarrassed me to read that as an adult. I wondered if I was a bully as a child. I also found some class pictures with a few people's faces scratched off. At first, I chuckled but then was saddened for my little self that I had felt such anger towards these people, one of whom I'm still friends with today. I had wished I hadn't done that. I wished I didn't have those mean thoughts in my head as a child.

But I'm not a child anymore. I'm an adult over 40 years later. My adult self is completely different from my child self. I did what I only knew how then. I reacted as I only knew how then.

I pulled myself out of this memory and wondered why my mind had been drawn in this direction. "What was that all about?" I asked myself, still staying at the heart chakra with this client. My higher self spoke of forgiveness to myself. You must forgive who you were, as that is not who you are today. I envisioned the cord between my adult self and my child self, and I proceeded to cut the cord between us. Those darn energy cords can hold us back from who we truly are today. I breathed deeper and felt like I was doing therapy on myself, all the while doing Reiki on this lovely client.

When our session was over, I mentioned to her about the heart chakra and how it felt so heavy and thick. She had noticed it too and was extremely tired after our brief 30 minutes. I felt a nudge from my higher self to tell her the story that happened to me. As I relayed how, as a child, I had regrets about how I acted and needed to forgive that past part of me, she nodded in agreement as that was exactly how she was feeling. I told her how to cut the cord between her and her past self (forgiveness). This entire experience was for both of our healing.

There is never a mistake who ends up on my table.

Especially with energy work. It is not just the client that is receiving the session.

I want to tell you another story about energy cords as this one made me believe that they really are present between us. About 10 years ago, one of my long term clients showed up for a massage. Carol was not her normal self this day. When I questioned her as to how she was, she proceeded to tell me about her horse, Covergirl. This horse was lame, limping around the yard, and just not herself. It was not enough to bring the vet out yet, but she feared she may need to put her down. We talked a bit more about the horse and then moved the conversation to how I could help her that day.

"Well", she said, "I have this hip pain and it's making me walk funny." "Interesting," I said as the lightbulbs were going off in my head. "What side is the horse limping on?" "It's the right side," she said, also noting the similarities. "Okay, let's back up again and tell me what this horse means to you?" She proceeded to say how it was one of her first horses, and they were very connected. She felt that this horse understood her and was always there for her. She has rode Covergirl for over 10 years.

This connection started when she first brought Covergirl home from Raleigh, North Carolina. Traveling with horses is intense and very stressful on them. By the time Carol had picked up Covergirl in North Dakota, she had already been traveling for 3 days. Covergirl was emaciated from the trip. There was nearly 10 more hours of travel to go. Instead of testing Covergirl's limits, Carol lovingly stopped traveling every hour to let her rest and give her water. This bond/cord likely started the moment Covergirl felt Carol's love and it was reciprocated.

I made her tell me about the connection as when we love something or someone and have a relationship with them, there is always an energetic cord. The stronger the relationship, the stronger the cord. This is especially true if one person in the relationship is the caregiver or is thought of as a 'saviour'. This wasn't completely true in this case, but their bond was strong. It is definitely something to watch in families and if you are a caregiver.

"Okay, let's cut the energetic cords between you and this horse", I exclaimed. "It's possible that you are both operating on each other's power. Our lives are meant to live on our own power. This won't hurt either of you, but will allow you to disconnect and stand in your own light."

I proceeded to lead her in the quick visualization (detailed below) and then we continued with her appointment. She left the office feeling pretty good. Three weeks later she came in again and said, "Cari, I forgot to tell you what happened last time I was in. I went home and my horse was running and jumping in the yard." Whaaaat!!! I couldn't believe it was that simple. Covergirl is still alive today, years later!

If you need to cut some cords between you and your younger self, or possibly with a relationship that is struggling or between you and anything that is leaking your power (maybe your horse), just follow this short visualization. You can cut cords daily or as you feel called. This is a great exercise to come back to throughout your life, especially if you work with people or kids.

Visualization to Cut Energy Cords

Take a couple deep breaths and just settle into your space. Allow your mind to guide you with this visualization. Let your soul know this is for your highest good only. In your mind, call in your 'team': guides, angels and ancestors to assist you.

Who in your life do you feel you may be sharing power with? Who do you feel may be taking your power or possibly, who are you tapping into and trying to take their power? Just allow your guides to show you who.

Now I want you to find the sharpest cutting tool that you would like to work with. This may be a knife, axe, machete, chain saw, what have you. With the help of your team, start cutting. See the cords returning to the person, see your body being free from all outside connections. When you feel it is complete, put your cutting tool down and invite in healing to your body. Thank your helpers for assisting you.

Feel free to do this little exercise when needed. You may get to the point where you will just need to command the cords to detach, and it will be so. When I do this, I use a commanding statement: "All energy cords that are attached to me or that I've attached to others need to drop and dissolve Now!" I say this daily as I work with people who sometimes think of me as the saviour who will fix all their problems. I love helping people but having lingering energy after a session is over is not desirable.

Play with it. It is a powerful way to operate solely on your own energy.

CHAPTER 16

CHAINS

What do you think of when you are at home sick? Where does your mind go when you are trying to fall asleep? I had quite an epiphany as I was repairing my body with some rest. The epiphany came as I was releasing attachments that were in or around my body in order for me to heal completely. I am very familiar with energetic cords as mentioned in the last chapter. I know about not being able to function to our true power as we draw from each other. But chains? This was new to me. This appeared in my consciousness, and I'd like to share it with you.

I was exploring how we put people and even ourselves on pedestals. We either think of others as greater than ourselves or less than. We put ourselves on these same pedestals thinking that I am something, because I have X, Y, and Z. Or, I have done this and that and so I am better than you. It's a bit comical when you start to think about it, but we have all done this.

Where did this come from? Who is teaching us that we are not all equal? Well, we are going to have to look way, way, back into history to find some origins. I'm sure it's not hard for you to see that race, governments, institutions, and even genders have given off this "I am better than you" vibe and then taught their children who taught their children. Be brave enough to have a look. Is this in your life, your family, or maybe your upbringing?

Since I was little, I had a gift of music. I started playing piano when I was 5 or 6. I enjoyed it, had an ear for it and became quite good at it. The people around me, family, friends, teachers, adjudicators etc., started noticing this talent and started praising me for it. This continued up into my twenties where I was involved in a touring music group and then various bands that played for audiences of hundreds at a time. I was good. Was I better than others? Well maybe my music ability was better than some, but I, as a person, was not any better than anyone.

The image of 'chains' came when I saw how others thought I was better than them. It also appeared when I saw others as better than me. Growing up, I had relatives that

I admired mostly because they were rich. The things their money could buy blew my mind, and I thought they were better than me. I formed a chain to them as I put them on a pedestal of greatness.

The chains appeared to go to others and attach to me as the levels of greatness and 'better than' appeared in my vision. I remember one chiropractor that I worked for fit this visual perfectly. He honestly took his hand and motioned above his head and said, "Chiropractors are here", then moved his hand lower, "Massage Therapists are here", and finally the lowest, "and our assistants are here." I remember laughing as that seemed so rude and judgmental in our place in the world. That is a chain. He put himself on a pedestal. Oh, my, how we have grown to understand things differently. Being a chiropractor is just a profession you have chosen as is an assistant. You are not any more special than the person who cleans the toilet. It is just a choice.

This will be visible in other places of life too; one just has to have a look. Think about the fascination people have with celebrities. (I love that it's starting to deplete.) Magazines are filled with what they are doing, wearing, and who they are with. I really can't believe anyone cares about that, but people do. Why do we care about them and not others?

When we put anyone on pedestals and attach a chain to them thinking they are greater than us, when they mess up, they really fall off the pedestal. It disrupts our thinking. This person who was greater just proved their human equality by falling down. The interesting thing is, no one helps them back up. In fact, just the opposite is true. We usually mock them and kick them while they are down. What is wrong with us?

I had an old teacher whom I respected, trusted, and truly admired for what she accomplished in life. I enjoyed learning under her, and I held her on this pedestal. Then, one day, she did a complete tumble off the pedestal. I couldn't believe her humanness was showing. I was astonished and saddened. I did kick her while she was down too. I was not conscious enough to know that I had put her in a higher place than myself. I had regarded her as greater than me.

I wonder if the world could grasp this thought that we may have more equality in all areas. The races have me baffled. This is a learned thought of being greater than another. It must be stopped and challenged. There is no race greater or less than another. We are all the same. There is no profession, status, culture, or human who deserves to sit on a pedestal. Wherever you have connected a chain to someone or possibly they have connected one to you, it's time to break them, for good! Just imagine a world of more equality. Imagine a world where we love ourselves enough to know we are equal to those we think highly of.

Thoughts to Ponder:

1. Who thinks of you as greater than/less than?
2. Who do you think of as greater than/less than?
3. Why do you think this of someone else?

CHAPTER 17

THE 8TH CHAKRA: COMMAND YOUR POWER

I love the chakras. They are the energy centers of the body. They hold an incredible amount of information for us to explore. Chakras tell a story of why we are feeling the way we are feeling physically, mentally, and even spiritually. I work with them the most in my energy work when reading a person's body and all the messages it wants to relay.

It was around 2021 that I heard more about the 8th Chakra and what it wanted to say to us. I was listening to the teachings of Bill McKenna, founder of Cognomovement, who opened my eyes to this new energy center. There is not a lot of information on it, but I would like to share some with you here. The other chakras (1-7) can be explored in my first book, *It's All About Energy*.

The 8th Chakra is called the Soul Star or Vyapini. It is positioned approximately a foot above the crown chakra. This chakra is all about the soul, represented by colors of gold or iridescence. The theme of this chakra is timelessness and heightened perception. It also represents stepping into our true purpose of why we are on the planet. It holds the place of our personal power that can be seen as arrogance if not kept in check.

If the 8th Chakra is unbalanced, it may also manifest as a disease or fear while a balanced expression brings about complete health (mind, body, spirit) and cosmic bliss. It sends messages urging us to connect with our higher selves, move away from the limitations of the mind, and open ourselves up to divine love.

Credit for these insights goes to various sources, including the teachings of Bill McKenna and especially Deborah King, who offers a deeper exploration of the chakras. According to King, when the 8th Chakra is in balance, we feel a profound alignment with our purpose, a connection to the broader world, and an intuitive clarity that guides our actions. An imbalance in this chakra may leave us feeling adrift, disconnected, or caught up in the ego.

For further exploration, have a look at Deborah King's insight into the 8th Chakra here: www.deborahking.com/5-things-you-need-to-know-about-your-8th-chakra/

An overactive 8th Chakra may give you the feeling of disconnection from the earth or feeling ungrounded. You may also experience a disconnection from your spiritual and physical self.

These last few sentences likely describe 90% of people on the planet. That's why this chakra is so important to look at. We are finally ready to as a species, as we are capable to understand it.

I cannot help you understand it. What I would love for you to do is to get that journal out and go on a visualization with me. If by chance you are reading these exact words on an evening with a clear sky, I'd like you to put your coat on and go and stand outside and look up.

Yes, have a look at the stars. For those of us reading in the daytime or are too lazy to go out, I want you to remember the last time you were able to look up at the blanket of stars. Got it?

The last time you saw the stars or are seeing them, how did/do you feel? What emotions or feelings come to you when you see these stars above you? Write that all down as it will help you make sense of this next section.

____

____

____

____

Some of the words used from students I have taught, and from my own feelings and emotions, include bright, wonderous, organized chaos, awe inspiring, peaceful, a perfect balance of light and dark, beautiful, safe, never ending, vast, makes me feel small yet a part of it all and so on. I hope you came up with a few descriptions of your own.

Did you know that you are stardust? Yes, flesh and blood are made of chemical elements including hydrogen, oxygen, carbon, nitrogen, iron, and other elements. Scientists estimate that 97% of the human body is composed of stardust. Isn't that interesting?

When you look up and see the stars, you are basically looking in a mirror of who you are. That's why I wanted you to describe the stars and realize that this is you. You may not even recognize these attributes in yourself, but they are there, otherwise you wouldn't have felt them, or seen them.

I know right! I was a little weirded out too when I first realized this all. Now looking up at the stars may be even a greater experience. So what does this all mean to our humanness? Why does having a balanced Soul Star (8th Chakra) matter? We will get to that but first I must share a story with you.

Years ago, my friend, Fay, and I were traveling to a spa in Kelowna, BC to lead a women's retreat. This was our second retreat ever that we organized. I believe we had about 8 women joining us the next day. We had a great weekend planned and were going the day before to get set up and ready for what was ahead. As we were about to board our second flight to the destination, the attendant said that there was a good chance the plane wouldn't land in Kelowna, rather we would be going to the nearest major airport, Vancouver (approximately 250 miles away).

I'm sure I looked like a deer in headlights as that was just not a good option for us. You know how you plan for everything, but there are just some things that you cannot even work around? This was one of them. Fay just demanded out loud "That's not happening." I was in a bit of a shock as all I could think about was how on earth we were going to prepare for the retreat this evening if we were in another city. The retreaters were probably having travel issues too. My mind started going into a logistical nightmare.

Fay took the lead and said to me and another retreater on that flight, "Okay, we are going to manifest this plane down." This is one thing I love about her is that she just knows what she wants, asks for it, and then gets to work manifesting.

The entire trip, I remember pretty much just meditating and praying that we would get this plane down. My prayers were a little like this: it would be really great if we could start the retreat on time and have everyone arrive safely. I was very meek and mild in my prayers and my manifesting. I had my eyes closed for the entire trip. It was less than an hour flight. We were above the city circling, but unable to land due to the storm below.

Suddenly, in my mind's eye, I saw this Zeus looking character who pounded his scepter into the ground and yelled at me, "Command your power!" I remember thinking, "Hmm, I wonder who you are… did I just witness that?" I kept on my meek and mild prayer, but maybe in a little stronger voice. BOOM!... Again this Zeus looking character shows up, pounds his little mermaid scepter, and says even louder, "Command your power!"

"He's getting intense," I remember thinking. I visualized us landing safely and repeated in my head that we ARE going to land. He showed up again and even louder and more forceful.

My human brain was thinking, "WTF, three times in a row. Is this vision for real? What is happening?" The plane is still circling, and the pilot has come on a couple times over the PA system saying he will circle until he either has enough gas to get to Vancouver or we are able to land.

I close my eyes again and keep praying, wondering if this is manifesting and what the heck these visions are. In my most stern inner voice that I ever asked with, I say, "This plane is landing and that's all there is to it." BOOM!

The PA system announces, "Ladies and gentlemen, please fasten your seatbelts and prepare for landing. I found a window in the storm and I am going to take it."

Holy shit! I looked at my friend and the fellow retreater and we just grinned. I felt like saying in my most Urkel voice (from the sitcom, Family Matters) “Did we just do that?”

Why am I telling you this story? Well, the 8th Chakra holds a huge message and it has to do with our power. This energy center is telling us to embody this power and it’s not in an arrogant way, but rather a direct, confident, command your power type of way.

This chakra wants us to step into the power that is inherently ours. This is a part of us. It’s who we are, but we may have forgotten (like so many things). Stepping into your power may have appeared throughout your life and possibly has been stifled by someone who doesn’t believe in their own power and feels they have to squash your power, so they feel good about where they are at.

For most of us, it’s true that there was no one in our world to show us what’s possible. There was no one to show us how to be powerful, but not arrogant or ignorant. Power on this planet is distorted and unnatural. It’s based out of fear and ruling people so that leaders can puff up their chest and make themselves feel better about themselves. It has nothing to do with the natural god given ability to be a powerful person in our own body, energy field and life. Are you ready to step into it?

Thoughts to Ponder:

1. Which attributes of the stars stick out the most for you?
2. What does power mean to you?
3. Do you know anyone who is powerful and not 'in your face' about it?
4. Will you command your own power and take this part of you back?

CHAPTER 18

I HATE THE WORLD TODAY

What started off as a Facebook post turned into so much more. I didn't say much. I just quoted this old song by Meredith Brooks and the comments started to fly. I think people were shocked that I have bad days. That's my fault for only expressing my good days to the public. I've never wanted to be a whiner or complainer, especially on social media, but this day and the days leading up to it, were hard.

It was 2020, more lockdowns were issued, and it was weighing on my clients as each one was coming in more depressed than the last with all the rules to live by. One 'rule', in particular, was the hospitals not allowing any visitors. This was a problem. My 94-year-old grandma was in there. My mom and sister were registered to be able to go see her prior to this new rule change. I hated not seeing her, but was so thankful someone could up until now. When this new rule happened, I was pissed. They didn't even let my mom in to tell my grandma why she wouldn't be back. There was a good chance their last visit already happened.

This same day, a friend and former massage therapist colleague messaged me and told me how they were getting shut down at work again just a province away. As you know massage therapy requires very close contact. This news put a little fear in me that this would be coming to our province. She only lived 90 minutes away. Did I mention this was all 2 weeks before Christmas?

I let my Facebook friends try to pick me up and with all their 'look on the bright sides', etc. They all meant well. My friend Randi said: "Cari, it's okay to be angry. Feel it, express it, and release it!" That resonated so loudly with me. My friend Shelly said, "Cari, where are you? I have something for you." She tracked me down and gave me a piece of birch tree, 5 ribbons, two sprigs of pine and a candle. She gave me the instructions of how to express and release. It was like these two were working together to help me heal, yet they had never met each other.

I get to work after purposely not filling my first client slot. I do listen to my own advice and take some 'me' time when needed. My first client was a worn-out teacher. She needed TLC and the timing of this massage was so divine in her life. It's an amazing reminder of how looked after we are. We ended the massage, and I sent her away with love and prepared for the next.

Second client comes in. "How was your day", I ask. "Horrible," she says! Yikes. We proceed to my massage room, and she tells me how a colleague had just died a couple hours ago. This colleague was best friends with my last client. Tears welled up in both of us and I asked her if I could hug her. (Yes, even hugs needed permission during this pandemic and many just never hugged.) She was sorry to have told me, but I was so thankful to have it come from a person and not read about it on social media. The person who passed was also a client. This really was turning into a horrible day. As she changed and got ready for the massage, I had a cry, prayed hard for my whole being to just get through this massage, to be a light, to be a relief of stress. It did work and it was just what she needed. I was so thankful to be able to help.

Later that evening my first client phoned me to let me know that this dear soul, her best friend had passed. We had a cry and I told her I loved her, something so unprofessional, yet it was necessary that day. It was such Divinity for her to have had a massage before getting that message. There is no other way to describe it. I'm so thankful that she shut her phone off during the massage. I'm so thankful that she didn't even pick up her messages in my room. She went home and her husband was there to hold her and grieve together.

I went home, poured myself a huge glass of wine and started to eat my meal. There was a knock at the door. So strange to hear a knock as we are all huddled in our homes with nowhere to go and be in the evenings. My financial advisor, Amanda, was standing in the doorway with her two boys. "I heard you were having a bad day and we wanted to drop off some cheer." She handed me this cute little wooden snowman and tells me her boys made it. "Oh my gosh, this is so sweet of you. I can't believe you made it and thought of me. Thank you so much!" I was quite overwhelmed by now with these unexpected things that kept happening. I felt like I was crying all day.

It doesn't end there. I'm playing on my phone, waiting for my wine buzz to kick in, and I get this message from an acquaintance who works in the hospital where my grandma was. I believe she is a senior nurse. She proceeds to tell me she saw my post on Facebook (I did have to explain to people why I was mad), and she thought there may be a loophole to have a look at. She said there was a meeting tomorrow about the patients and she will advocate for our family. And I'm bawling again! I thanked her profusely and she said she would try and let my mom know in the morning.

One little social media post produced a massive reach out of concern! I told my husband that maybe I should complain a little more in life.

This day taught me so much about expressing ourselves, about how we are all so connected and how just reaching out can mean so much. I didn't tell you about all the people who sent me a private message to ask how I really was. It seriously makes a difference to be real, to let people see a side of you that is vulnerable, to hold each other when there is nothing else to say. I feel extremely fortunate for these people in my life who took their time to reach out.

Thoughts to Ponder:

1. Have you ever given yourself permission to have a bad day and let others see?

2. Do you hide behind a 'happy face', making people believe you have super-powers for not feeling what you really feel?

3. What would life be like if you did let people know your true feelings? Would the world crumble around you or would you feel more human?

CHAPTER 19

FREEZE

Our body has a fight or flight system. I know it well. I know what happens with the body physiologically and how this has evolved from our ancestors. It wasn't until recently that I begun hearing about the fight, flight or freeze system. I had never been taught the third response that our body has. Once it was explained to me, the light bulbs were blasting off in my head!

When an animal or a human has a threat of danger, there really are three responses, not two. We can fight, we can run and take flight, or we can freeze. Now, why would you ever want to freeze? I always thought this is what you do when you see a bear (of which I have a fear growing up in the bush), but you really don't want to freeze for a black bear. You grow as large as you can and slowly walk backwards. You basically take 'controlled' flight and hope to hell it doesn't chase you. If it does, you should fight it, especially on the nose. Pray that it's not too hungry. But do not freeze! So, when would a person or animal freeze?

If a tiger is chasing a herd of goats and one just happens to fall from the pack and it knows it has no chance to fight the tiger or run from the tiger, it freezes. Now it does this for a couple reasons. Supposedly the body actually dies (likely from fear) and the animal doesn't feel the pain. The goat's body can also come back to life. If the tiger just happens to drag it to another area to feast on later, the goat may just run away. I have never seen this happen, but when I think about it, have you ever seen this with a fly? You whack it and moments later it flies away? Did it practice the freeze technique for survival? Oh, the things that make me go hmm!

During Covid, possibly like you, I was forced off work for 8 weeks as it's impossible to massage someone from two meters away. During this time off (which I should have celebrated, but it was just so weird and unpredictable, and no one could go anywhere), I found myself freezing! I would curl up on the couch in the fetal position and listen to a meditation and just cry. I had no idea why; it would just happen. I could not run from Covid; I could not fight it. All I could do was freeze. Was this the survival response that got me through it? This time of our history was extremely stressful for everyone. Brilliant me…I could also feel the collective stress that I believe was causing this response in my body.

I have projects on the go right now, but I still find myself freezing. I find myself not knowing how to motivate myself to move into something different. Animals, like the goat, they just find their opportunity and run away. They either get eaten by the tiger who awakens, or they find their flock and just keep moving on. As a human, we have conditions that we give ourselves for this type of response: Post-traumatic stress disorder (PTSD) or generalized anxiety disorder (GAD) or acute stress disorder (ASD). Us humans are so advanced that we have labels and drugs and therapy for our stressors. Don't get me wrong, I'm glad there is help out there, but why does it get stuck in the body? Why can we just not move on like the goat?

It's our brain. Our thoughts get in the way and create the stress over and over. We think about it and can't stop thinking about it, and it paralyzes us. There is nowhere to move, because we can't. We stay in the loop of it! We keep reliving the trauma.

I wonder how much less the goat thinks? Does the goat only know to live in the moment? Does the goat even know it has other choices? Does it know it could live in the past and relive it every day, or fantasize about the future and live there too? Is living moment to moment our salvation out of all these disorders? How does one just discard what has happened in our past? It happened; it sucked! Do we just stop living it and be here, be now? That seems too simple.

What can I choose now, knowing that I am the creator of my life? I choose to examine it. I choose to learn from it. I choose to have it be a part of my life, but not have it control me. It's the same as that damn virus. It is a part of our life, our history, and has affected every single aspect of it. Do we let it control us? I declare today that all my past hurts and stress responses no longer have control over how I want to live my life. I choose to move forward and as close to 'in the moment' as possible.

Thoughts to ponder:

1. What is your stress response? (Fight, Flight or Freeze)

2. Can you remember how and when you have used this response?

3. Has it served you well or hindered you from living more fully?

CHAPTER 20

THE ENERGY OF CHANGE

Have you seen the cartoon of the two butterflies? One is fully developed with beautiful wings and the other one is still a green worm. The worm says, "You've changed!" The butterfly says, "You're supposed to." That says everything about life. I am around people daily who are afraid of change. People who are thinking that what they have now is all there is. Also, people who are satisfied and do not want any more change in their life. They are done; they have had enough. Change was not as kind to them as it was to the butterfly.

With my career as a business owner, the observation I

have seen continuously is that those who are comfortable with change, tend to be the most successful, less stressed, more optimistic people that I have worked with. They have learned how to adapt. How did they do that?

Change is very uncomfortable. It contains the entire element of the unknown. All the what-ifs can be overwhelming. So much so that it often talks a person out of something new and different. If you look around at the world's history or even at nature, change is everywhere! How did we become so afraid of it?

I believe it has a lot to do with how we were shown change. Did you grow up in a family where your parents had the same job for their entire work life? Maybe they lived in their home for your entire childhood. Maybe they had the same friends or ate the same food each week. Possibly you took one vacation a year to the same place. Did you really experience any change? What is change? Did anyone ever show you how to walk through a wall of change? Maybe you have only seen change as a negative thing such as when someone passes away and the whole world changes for them?

One of the easiest ways to get comfortable with change is to try new things. Even if it's a new dish for your evening meal. This can start to encourage small change. Going to the hair salon and asking for a new do can be a part of change. Moving to a new community, changing jobs, or enrolling in school can be a change. Why is this even necessary to purposely evoke change which can be stressful?

Why not continue to do what you have always done?

In my 30s and 40s I traveled a lot. I loved it and truly miss it, as I'm writing here in 2022 (still recovering from the world being shut down). When visiting another country, it was so fun to check out their sites, their local cuisine, and to see what their landscape was all about. It opened my eyes and my heart to how other people live. I was curious about their lifestyle and their day-to-day activities. This experience expanded my outlook on life. I could see things differently.

When a person sees someone doing something, they know it is possible for them too. A local business owner has told me a few times, "I saw you running your business and told myself 'I can do that!'" Yes, you can! Changing how you live, how you look, how you work, etc… we can all do that. Sometimes it just takes someone to show us what is possible.

The courage to change is the next step. You can possibly see what you want, but how do you muster up the drive to get there? Especially if you have never been there before. (I encourage you to stop here and go plug in the song 'Courage to Change' by Sia. Crank it!)

There is another very important element to change. It stimulates your brain. In the chiropractic workshops that I have been invited to, they talk about brain health and how change is important for its health. This was further encouraged with my Cognomovement training. After each set of this modality, we even change positions in the room as the brain gets so familiar with its environment that it starts to do the same things over and over rather than helping a person get from A to B in life. The brain gets used to the pattern that we create for it, and it can lead to stagnation. The chiropractors talked about how changing up a picture in your house or driving a new way to work will encourage change in the brain. When we get familiar with our environment, we can get a little stuck.

Another observation of change is that when a person starts working on themselves and change starts to happen, many more things in life can also start to change. At the time I am writing this, I have gone through a year of learning about brain health and change and have worked through some of my own blocks and traumas. As they start to clear, change is happening all around me. We are doing a major renovation in our house. I just cut 5 inches off my hair. My hubby and I are both thinking about our next career move. Huge change is coming in our lives. We started playing with change and inviting it in and now it has shown us what else is possible. We have two choices here. Embrace it or be afraid of it and stop it all from happening. My curious soul just wants to see where it will take us, even though we have had some very uncomfortable conversations and thoughts of 'what-if!'

The energy of change holds all the possibilities for life. A tree changes through all the seasons. I look out onto my own property to be reminded of this. Even in the season of death (huge change), the tree accepts this part of its cycle. Can we?

Thoughts to Ponder:

1. What can you do today to create just a little change to shake up your comfort level?
   (Redesign something in your home? Paint a wall? Cook something different? Change your hair or wardrobe?)

2. Are you afraid of change? How can you become more comfortable with it?

3. Have you ever stunted your own human growth because you were afraid of change? What happened? Where were you? Would you like to try it now?

CHAPTER 21

SPIRIT AND HUMANNESS

I am fortunate to take a break, at least once a year, and venture to a spa. If you have never experienced spa life, you really need to look some up. Sometimes I call myself a spa whore! I have been to most of Canada's major spas and a few amazing ones out of country. This weekend I am at a spa in Comox, BC, Canada, and it is quite glorious. I am needing some time to recharge my batteries. My life hasn't been that hard or troublesome lately, but the people around me have spilled their stories and I can't help but feel all the feels. It's draining.

I wish I didn't feel sometimes, but I do. I feel everything. I've tried so many tips and tricks to not feel for another person and yet I do. I am almost shamed in the energy community for still feeling hardships from clients because according to many 'gurus' I don't have to. Am I choosing to then? Why do I sometimes cry with my clients in the room when they are telling me about their partner dying or a dog they had to put down? Why can't I just look at them stone faced and not feel that loss?

What a question for me? Am I choosing this or just being a human? Can some people shut it off and turn it on? Are some people even capable of feeling things and some not? Can a person really be human and not feel anything? So many questions.

The day before my grandmother died, it was her 75th anniversary. She was not herself this day and later we assumed she had possibly had a mini stroke. I asked her, "Grandma, how do you feel today?" She said to me, "Cari, I don't feel anymore."

That struck me as odd, but today it may just be the insight I am pondering. Little did we know that was the last day we would be able to communicate with her. She died the next evening. Was she already partly gone and in spirit? Do we feel when we are in spirit?

When I say 'in spirit' I mean detached from our humanness because our 'spiritness' is always with us. There is this game I play with myself about humanness and spirit. Kind of like 'what would Jesus do' but more 'this is what my human side would do, and this is what my spirit side would do.' When we are a spirit living in a human body, we are going to be and do both. I don't believe there is another way unless that will be revealed to me one day.

Here's an example of what I'm trying to say, in case I've completely lost you. A few days ago, I came across a last name which was also the same last name as the woman who had a huge part in breaking up my first marriage. For shits and giggles, I decided to look up this said woman on the world wide web and, lo and behold, she was right there staring back at me. Right away I felt anger towards her and may have called her a bitch all over again. I relived those dark days and nights with her in our life. The breakup wasn't all about her, but she was a massive instigator. My humanness showed emotions of anger, pain, and sadness just by seeing her face, and seriously, I've been divorced for 25+ years already. Why am I still feeling things?

I gave my head a shake and asked my spirit what it had to say. What a laugh! It was a complete opposite of what was going on in this 3D humanness. My spirit knew she was a gift and an instigator for me to become what I needed to be in this world. Without her in my first marriage, it likely would have lasted longer and I would be in misery. I would have played the game of 'happy wife' which wasn't so happy as I wasn't living my true authentic self. (Have I mastered true authenticity? Do we ever?) Spirit knows and shows a different game in life than our humanness does. You have all heard the saying about being a spirit in a human body. This means we have two sides to us, always, at all times.

So yes, I would like to not feel for these people. That is my humanness… feeling. My spirit knows that I am always in the right place at the right time and if I can serve in any way, I will. If my human life can help ascend another's, so be it. That is the message of the spirit. The spirit holds no attachment and has no feelings towards a human. A spirit just is and just be's.

Now if I live my life more in the spirit, will I have the same attachments unto others? Likely not. Is that desire or a plan for us? I'm not even sure yet. I say that because we chose to come back here as a human with our spirit. We are going to have human experiences. We are going to have human feelings. We are going to have human attachments. All because we are human. When those attachments get too overwhelming, we must remember that we are also spirit. It sure puts a different spin on hardship and stress.

Looking at death through spirit's eyes is very different than from human eyes. The spirit celebrates death as that is when we return to our natural state, who we really are. If you have ever been in the room when someone dies, consider it a blessing as they were comfortable enough for you to be there. The one dying also knew you would be okay with the experience, even if that takes a long while for some. If you are ever fortunate enough to watch the spirit leave the body, it's very magical and surreal. Our spirit celebrates. Our humanness mourns.

Many of us are good at living in just the human world. Some label this as being unconscious and unawakened. It makes me wonder if living in the spirit world full time is possible while we are on the planet. Likely not, until we drop off our human bodies. While we have a human body, we need to experience all that we can – pleasure, pain, love, and loss – until one day you do not feel again and return fully back to spirit.

Thoughts to Ponder

1. If you believe you are spirit, what are you doing to nurture your spirit?
2. Are you making this a priority in your life?

PART 3

DEATH

The fear of death follows from the fear of life. A man who lives fully is prepared to die at any time.

- Mark Twain

CHAPTER 22

THE DEATH OF YOU

What a morbid title to a chapter. Death in all its meaning is something no one really talks about, especially if it pertains to you. Why would you want to talk about your own death? Why wouldn't you? We are all going to die.

My husband and I had a great conversation one day after a loved one's funeral. We started planning our own funerals. Both of us don't want to drag our friends to a church service, you know the kind where they use the death of a loved one to try to preach the gospel and lead you to Christ. What a crazy way to be an evangelist, yet some people opt for this way and well, to each their own. It feels to me like the preacher is saying "See, this could happen to you, and where will you go? Heaven or hell?"

No, I want a party. I want people to celebrate my life. If I have impacted them in any way, I want them to dance and laugh and eat and drink. Why not celebrate the fact that we met, knew, and loved each other in whatever way? I saw a Facebook video taken from a woman's funeral. People were gathered and looking their somber selves, when suddenly, a flash mob starts dancing. Could you imagine hiring a dance crew to lighten up your funeral? This was in a church no less. You should have seen the people's reactions to this spontaneous disruption to their mourning faces. The song was 'Another One Bites the Dust.' It was hilarious to the observer (as someone who has no connection to the woman who had passed). Still, some who may have been in mourning likely didn't appreciate the lightness of the dance. This was the exact point of the deceased. Lighten up, it's only death.

"Oh, Cari, are you off your rocker, only death? Death is massive and painful and sad."

Is it?

Where does that belief come from? Has this been your only experience?

The first time I really watched death was with my fabulous father-in-law. I didn't have long to get to know him.

He passed about 8 years after we met. He was a straight shooter and told things like it was, even if it was crass and politically incorrect. He passed that gene on to his son quite nicely. He often didn't have a filter and that was one of the things I loved about him most. He was real.

He came to visit one summer, and we started noticing that he wasn't enjoying his favorite things. Coffee wasn't as tasty to him or the traditional beer and clam we would share while barbecuing. It made us all pause and go hmmm. It took only a month from there to be called to his bedside in the hospital in the middle of the night. You know those nights you remember because you are forever changed? This was one of them.

I was at our family cabin that night. We had just arrived, and I was getting ready for bed. I decided to call my husband and check in to see if he had heard from his mom regarding his dad. Craig sounded sad and scared, and we talked to calm each other, as we knew what was happening and it was so out of our control. After hanging up, I didn't feel right and decided to go back to town to be with my hubby.

We finally got settled into bed and the dreaded call came. "You must come." We packed a bag and drove the 90 minutes to the hospital. I remember putting the bag in the trunk and looking up at the stars on the quiet night and for some reason thinking "tonight is going to change you."

We arrived at the hospital filled with family. They told us

it wouldn't be long before he was gone, and my beautiful lifeless father-in-law likely waited for us to arrive before he departed. As the family all said goodbye to him and left, we decided to stay up and sit by his side. Craig and I held his hand, and I closed my eyes and started to pray. I remember Craig saying, "Cari, what are you doing?" He likely thought I was falling asleep, and he didn't want to be alone in case something happened. His mom was getting settled to rest in a chair close by. I told him that I was just praying. "Well, pray out loud," said the man with no filter.

And so I did, "Darle, thank you for being a father to us. May you be greeted by your loved ones and angels as you walk into this next part of life. Don't worry about us, we will take care of each other. I pray for the peace that surpasses all understanding for you and all of us." It was literally moments later that he experienced his last breath, and my life was forever changed, just as the stars had said.

To be able to witness death is a precious gift. Now I can also go into my humanness and tell you about all the tears and grief that myself and the family experienced. I can tell you how hard it was to go back to the house and tell my nephews. I can tell about how exhausted we all were and how lost we all felt. That is all the human response to death of a loved one. It is not wrong; it just is, and it is okay.

The spirituality of death is one of the most beautiful events that will take place in our life. For most people, this isn't what we look at. Instead, our humanness looks at the loss. We will be returning to source, back to our real home, to our original state of being. Truthfully, I can hardly wait! When the time has come for us to say good-bye to the struggle of being human, I will welcome it with open arms. The pain of existence physically, mentally and emotionally will be gone; no more worries or fighting to survive. Complete peace will overtake us. This is what I have seen with my loved ones and what we have heard from the other side.

Oh yes, I still communicate with my loved ones even though they have dumped off their physical bodies. In fact, my father-in-law, Darle, was the first to come through and continues to visit every now and then.

The first time the visits happened was when my friend invited me to her house a couple months after Darle passed. She had a guest in who was talking to the angels. For some reason, in my head I thought she said, "about the angels", and I thought "Cool, I'd like to learn about angels more". Well, she had invited a medium in to get the messages from the other side to the loved ones who gathered. I wanted to run! What did I get myself into? I decided to stay out of not wanting to look foolish and rude.

Darle was the second or third reading that day. The medium was describing this man who sounded exactly like my father-in-law, yet I didn't want to admit it or even make eye contact. Well, these spirits are so smart. He stood beside me, and the medium saw who he was connected to and called me out. I burst into tears. She then delivered the messages to me and my husband. He told us that he is good and checks in on us all the time. He touches my husband's left side to let him know that he is there. He told us that our business is getting bigger (which it did). It was like having a cup of coffee with him, so natural, and yet how could this be?

Darle made a few appearances to me and even to Craig. It seems like he can still father from afar. I did have a funny experience with him while cooking. I wasn't thinking about him or anything, then he appeared and told me he missed the taste of bacon. Of course, I was like "Where did that come from?" I sensed him and had a little laugh and continued on.

He showed himself to Craig one crazy night as life was shifting in the career department. Craig noticed that our lights kept flickering as he was making this huge decision about where to work after a fall out with a colleague. I'm so glad that, prior to this event, Craig had heard all my 'crazy talk' and recognized that this was strange and likely someone wanting his attention. In his full awareness he said, "I think my dad is here."

To further calm him down that night, after a little walk to clear the air, Craig found $5 in a mud puddle. He never takes things as signs, except that night. He knew he was being looked after. He felt a fatherly presence and knew it was going to be okay.

When we are quiet enough and aware enough, we will feel, sense, hear or know that our loved ones are still around.

They are likely having the time of their life! I often wonder if I will haunt people when I'm gone?

If we are still here after our physical death, what really is there to be afraid of or scared of? Possibly you have never looked at this to even see through the fear. This to me is the death of ourselves. When you can die to this thought of the absolute end is when the body dies, you will live. It's time to live.

We put all this attention on the physical form while here on the planet when really, we should be evolving our soul as this is all that matters in the end.

Will you choose to evolve, or will you choose to get lost in this human game?

Look a little deeper into life and in the struggle of the humanness you will find the spiritual bliss of who you really are. You will find you, an energetic, spiritual being, having a human experience. When you die to the thought of your humanness, true living can begin. When you awaken to your energetic and spiritual being, you can exist in this world knowing that it's only a temporary stop into something far beyond this worldly life.

Thoughts to Ponder:

1. Have you been visited from a loved one? Possibly you have sloughed it off and thought that's not possible. What happened?

2. What do you believe happens to you after you die physically? What do you believe about death?

3. What are you doing to evolve your spirituality?

CHAPTER 23

CALLING IN THE ANCESTORS

Those who know me know of my love for travel. I have been to many countries and desire to visit many more. The richness you receive by enjoying another culture has no comparison to anything else you will experience in this life.

I have never been so aware of our ancestors as on my trip to the Big Island of Hawaii. I was participating in a Healer's Mastermind Retreat with Bonnie Bogner leading our group. This entire experience was all about following my intuition. My husband didn't want to travel that winter. My body did. I found this retreat and inquired about it. I was a little late for the registration cut off, and Bonnie was about to cancel the entire thing. The day I registered, two others did as well, and so the retreat was suddenly back on. I love it when these things happen as it confirms to me that they were meant to be.

I didn't know anyone on the retreat, including Bonnie. I had only heard of her. Somehow this didn't matter. I was going to Hawaii (favorite place on the planet) and learning about the things that interest me, with people who have a similar mindset.

The day of travel to Hawaii arrived. My excitement was so strong, yet I was a bit nervous as it had snowed the night before. I knew the plows wouldn't have been out yet. I had a three-hour drive in the dark and through the forest that I wasn't looking forward to. I kissed my husband and held my kitties, and out the door I went into this void, off to the airport. As I drove out of town, the highway became one lane. I had allowed for plenty of time to get to the airport but never expected a cow path to the city. I was a bit nervous and honestly, if it were for any other event other than travel, I would have turned around in a heartbeat. The early hour was a saving grace with no traffic, but it also was a curse with no snowplows out.

My mind played the dance. "I should turn around. Keep going. Turn around. Keep going." I became confused and more nervous. Suddenly, I could see in my mind's eye, smell the cologne of, feel and hear my father-in-law, Darle, who had passed a few years ago now, say, "Keep going Cari.

We will get you there." Okay, now I have tears in my eyes, which didn't help with the driving situation. His presence was so palpable that I felt he was in the passenger seat. He had shown up before with the smell of his cologne to let me know he was there. Today was no different and I could smell him beside me in the car, and he brought the others. On a side note, my father-in-law didn't wear cologne very often, but he did when he was around loved ones for weddings and funerals or special events.

Anyone who doesn't recognize this part of life would likely have been freaked out and possibly driven in the ditch. My body relaxed, somehow knowing that I was being looked after, and it confirmed I was supposed to be going to this retreat. The roads eased up after a couple of hours of white-knuckle driving. My only question through all of this was that Darle said, "We will get you there." I wondered who else was helping?

I made it to the airport with a heavy sigh of relief. The first leg of my travel was complete. Now I could rely on the pilots to do the rest.

After nearly 24 hours of car, plane, plane, plane, and van rides, I arrived exhausted and ready to sleep. I'd made it. I was in Hawaii. I was in my happy place. Oh, what great things were in store for me now?

The 10 days zoomed by as they always do when you are having fun. We ended up going to a spiritual gathering, like church, but different. As the speaker welcomed us all there, he said that there were many others that wanted to be with us today. Then he passed the microphone around and told us to state which of our ancestors who have passed were with us or that we would like to be with us. This little exercise took a bit of time as there were close to 100 people there, each one of us taking time to welcome our ancestors.

When it got closer to my turn, I started to sense the occupancy of the room. There were many more than 100 people there. I could feel the presence of the loved ones, which made it feel like 200 plus. It was very warm, inviting, supportive and loving.

My turn came and I asked my Grandma Moffet to come. She had appeared to me in mediumship readings before. She is a silent source of strength.

This entire experience was meaningful and not forgotten throughout my time in Hawaii. But that wasn't the last time my ancestors would appear on this island trip.

One of the days in our rented house by the ocean, I connected with a local massage therapist for an afternoon of bliss. I love receiving massage when I travel. It's fun for me to see what other therapists do. She was Hawaiian and so pleasant and kind. When she was ready, she ushered me into the room, gave me the instructions and left me to get undressed. When she came back in, she gently placed her hands on my body and said, "Now we will invite in the ancestors. Is that okay?" Oh, yes! My entire being responded. She began chanting and singing in Hawaiian.

It was so beautiful. It felt different than any session I had ever had before. Before she left the room after the massage ended, she prayed a blessing and kissed my head.

The last part of this ancestral story is back in my own treatment room after all this experience with calling in our loved ones. Now, before my own client arrives and sometimes during the session, I will call in their ancestors to assist and support in love. I find since I have been doing this, the client relaxes faster and deeper. It's almost like how you would trust a family member more than a stranger. You trust faster because you know them. I also believe that when a loved one is on the other side assisting, they only do so in kindness. I only ask for ancestors who can assist out of love, just in case I call in someone who does the opposite. I'm not even sure that could happen, but I'll take a precaution.

This one late afternoon my regular client came in and asked for her usual treatment. We do about 75 minutes of massage and 15 minutes of Reiki. She comes in to rebalance and keep her going. This night in particular, I asked her guides and ancestors to come and be with her, to let her receive what she needs for her highest good. She was very restless and had a hard time relaxing. Little did I know, until after, that she kept seeing her loved ones. They were coming to her. It made her pay attention as she was realizing that she wasn't asking for their help as often as she used to. When I told her that I called them in, she was a bit taken aback. Not in a bad way, just a little astonished as she had a hard time relaxing, because their faces were so vivid.

I believe they were trying to get her attention and I look forward to seeing what transpired after she connected with them.

Call in your loved ones to help. They are there for us and need an invitation. Talk to them as though they are physically present, even if it's in your mind. This is an especially good thing to do if you have unresolved issues with a loved one who has passed away. Connect with them and speak your mind. Get all the issues out of your body so that you can live in peace. You deserve peace.

You may get the sense that their spirit is much different from the human life they lived. You may even step into forgiveness. There are many great mediums out there that will connect with your loved ones. Healing conversations can be had and speaking your mind can also still happen.

As I have grown older and examined my life and my beliefs, I have concluded for me that when this body dies, the spirit lives. We are body, mind and spirit. We come to the planet to have a human experience. Therefore, we are still able to reach out to our loved ones. They just don't have a body anymore and are likely happy about that!

Thoughts to Ponder:

1. Who would you love to have a conversation with who has passed away?

2. Do you have unresolved issues with someone who

has passed away? Would you like to connect?

3. What is your method for sensing their presence: feeling, seeing (mind's eye), hearing, knowing, smelling or some other way?

CHAPTER 24

THE JOY OF SADNESS

It was a midweek party. My grandparents were being celebrated. All of us wondered how two people could share 75 years together. We watched them hold hands, look into each other's eyes, smile for our pictures, and, of course, eat cake. My grandma was in a senior's home, and we took my grandpa there for visits. Today we gathered outside, under the trees with the birds singing, to celebrate and admire their life together.

It was just over 12 hours after the party that the call came that my grandma had a stroke in the night and was unresponsive. This was likely it. We were prepared as much as we could be. She was 95 and had a very full life. She had people around her who loved her. She was being well cared for. The most comforting thought for me was that she wanted to die. We had talked about it so many times.

She often wondered why she was still alive. This would almost bother her when she heard of someone younger than her who had passed. When her body could no longer do what she wanted it to do, she longed to see what was on the other side for her. She had a deep faith in Jesus and was not afraid to meet him.

I visited her lifeless body that morning. I held her hand for the last time and tried to sing to her through my tears. She was such an amazing grandma. I felt such gratitude as we spent our last earthly moments together. She was like my second mom. She anticipated my birth and now, here I sat, anticipating her death. I said goodbye, I thanked her and wondered so graciously where she was going. "Come and see me in my dreams, Grandma."

The timing of this day was complete perfection. All who were at the party the day before shuffled in one by one to say their final good-byes. Her body stayed alive for each one, yet was unresponsive.

I managed to work that day. I did not talk about it to anyone in fear I may break down. I went home in sadness to prepare some food and then would go to the bedside.

As I was cooking my dinner, I found myself singing. She

loved music and loved to sing herself, especially when she was younger. Her favorite song was playing on my phone, the one she wanted at her funeral; the one I knew I would never be able to sing to her. So, I sang it now, in my kitchen with no one around.

During this exact time, my mom texted me. "It won't be long" is all she said. I dropped my knife and turned off the burner and shot through the door. It was only a 2 minute drive from my house. I flew in her room, took one look at Grandma, and knew she was gone. I changed my gaze to my mom and held her hard as we cried together. Slightly composed, we sat. I grabbed my grandmother's lifeless hand and exclaimed: "You did it, Grandma. I'm so happy for you!" Laughter and tears filled the room. My sister arrived and, with her too, we celebrated the passing. How can we be so joyful? It nearly rocked us to recognize how happy we were for her. This is what Grandma wanted more than life itself, and therefore we celebrated her.

Divine timing was the theme to her passing. She loved to gather and share food all through her life. Our Covid capacity restrictions on large gatherings had just been lifted and we were able to have a traditional funeral as she wanted. Family arrived and we visited and ate, just like Grandma would have wanted.

There is joy in passing. It is very subtle, and one must look sometimes to find it. If you have only experienced sadness around death, you may not have seen its glimpse. The body is showing itself to me as this clump of energy and it's inside of us. We are more than our body and we, our energy, extends further out from our body. When we die, it is only this mass of energy (the body) that dies. The spirit, or energy field is still there. I believe, therefore, when we call upon our loved ones for help, the energy can be felt because it can never die. This little thought helps me process my grief: she is still here; only the body has left.

About three weeks after my grandma's passing, I was having lunch with my highly intuitive friend, Vicki. She had just given me a session and helped me restore some of my own energy. Now we were catching up with some yummy Mexican food. In mid-sentence Vicki stopped what she was saying and received a message from my grandma that brought more tears. She said, "Cari, you already know this, but your grandma is here around you, and wants me to tell you that she is so thankful that you are still talking to her, because no one else in the family is. They all think she is really gone." Oh, Grandma, thank you for that confirmation.

Thoughts to Ponder:

1. What are your thoughts on death? What do you believe happens when a body dies?

2. Have you had conversations with your loved ones about when they pass away?

3. Of the loved ones who have passed away in your life,

who would you love to have a conversation with? Sit with yourself, find some silence and maybe a journal or cup of tea and just start thinking about them and talk to them. See what your experience is.

Sweet Sadness

by Tara Semple

How can sadness be so sweet?
Is it where Soul's sorrow meets?
Buck Moon sheds light on spiritual ground
Parting lips, inner risings, sound.

Open arms receive moon shining
Frozen heart with silver lining
Hear the call of Heartbeats' rhythm
Dancing with our long past visions.

Listen deeply to her call
Removing layers, letting fall
Naked in our own true nature
Learning of our Earth's Creator.

The sounds start softly, sit still, surrender
Rocking, cooing always tender
Melody, Harmony all in the circle
Life's for living, not a rehearsal.

Taste the sweetness of succulent sorrow
Take a bath in Life's tomorrow
Find the gold in Nature's cracks
We will find, no longer lacks.

Even in sadness, life's joy slips in
Always Yang as part of Yin
Reach for the stars, know playing in sand
Enjoy each day's fullness, living each strand.

This poem was exactly how I felt about my grandmother's passing. It had to be added and I'm so thankful for poets like Tara who capture our feelings in words.

To see more of Tara's work, you can check out:
https://shunyatasoundstudio.com/

CHAPTER 25

THE ENERGY OF DEATH

My grandfather died a few weeks ago. His death hit me hard and I'm still experiencing the waves of grief. Of course, I am. It doesn't just disappear when the funeral is held. Sometimes these waves last years or a lifetime. My grandpa was one of the most special relationships I have ever had.

He knew me from the time I was born, although he didn't recall any details from my birth. My grandma caught them all in her diary which I have.

"May 26, 1973: Jack took Pauline to the hospital at 7:30am. Baby was born at 8:30pm."

What an amazing thing to see your birth documented. Even if there was no emotion expressed, it's super cool to see what all happened after I was born, too. I had my first bath in June, and I had already went camping in July.

From reading my grandma's words, I saw how I was at their place weekly and saw them nearly daily while growing up. Through my teens and twenties, they were there, this steadfast force. They were always supportive, even if they didn't agree with what I was doing or what I believed. They were there!

After my grandma died, I tried to be as supportive as I could to my grandpa. I really can't believe he lasted as long as he did. Imagine, being married to someone for 75 years and then, for the first time in your life, as you turn 100 years of age, you are alone. Likely his spirit wanted to experience living alone, but not for long as he chose to leave too. It was quite the adventure to watch.

Shortly after my grandma's funeral, I started seeing her in my dreams. Her and I were in a line to go roller skating and she was so young and happy. She was with a friend and so was I. That was a funny dream, filled with so much joy.

The next dream was her showing me how to vacuum. This one seemed much more her style as she always had her house neat, tidy, and clean. I felt so happy that she came to see me, even if it was to give me vacuum lessons! These dreams were very real.

Days before my grandpa passed, I could tell that he was both in this world and in the next. He had told me months prior that he thought he was done, that he was ready to go. There is such sadness for our humanness in this moment. "I don't want you ever to leave. You have been my constant for nearly 50 years. Can't you stay forever?" That is what I wanted to say, instead I said, "Okay, Grandpa. I honor that, and I will support you until the end." We also talked about how lucky he was that he could go, and his time was very near.

As he laid in his bed in the hospital, a couple of family members caught him conducting a choir. "Do you hear the music," he said to my mom. "No, there is no music playing." "Yes, there is, but they are quite off tune," he replied. She laughed it off, but then her and my brother-in-law both saw him conducting. He loved music, and I wish we could hear what he was witnessing.

"Cari, I saw two angels in my room," he said one day. "Really", I replied all excited, "are they here now?" "No, they are gone now. Do you believe me?" He looked me in the eyes. "Absolutely, I believe you, Grandpa!" I meant every word. Then, I wanted to tell the angels to stay away as I knew exactly what was happening.

It was a Monday, and he was still of sound mind. His body was deteriorating but he was still with us, giving us advice in life. He joked around even and had such a good day that he mentioned to a family member, "I guess I'll stick around for one more day." Saying good-bye to him this day was so hard. He would always say to me, "Cari, if I don't see you here", and point to his bed, "I'll see you there", and point to the sky. I cried and he just looked through me. It was as though his emotions no longer affected him.

I noticed this with my grandma too, when she was close to passing over. Such an interesting thing to note. It is us who are feeling EVERYTHING. They are becoming more and more at peace and 'one' with their spirit, as well as with what is happening.

The next day my grandpa was super restless. He had company all day and family sat with him, sang to him, and even prayed with him. I could not go. It was too sad for me to be in his presence. I decided to stay home. It wasn't even a hard decision and I do not regret it. For months now, I had said all I needed to say to my grandpa. We always ended each visit with a hug and an "I love you." We were good and I knew how to find him, should he pass.

Well, he was true to his word. When all the company had finally left him, he passed in his sleep. I sure wonder what that experience is like. We had talked about it a lot. He was strong in his Christian faith and so he based what was to come on what the bible says. Even the bible cannot know what really is to come. If man wrote the bible, how on earth would they know what the other side is like?

The day of his passing I feel like I cried more than I ever had for someone who has gone. It was so strange that his death was the one that really got me. I do believe that I was also mourning my grandma. The time with them in my life is over. How do I move on?

It was decided that my husband and I would still go on our planned holiday the day Grandpa passed. I took my laptop and would help my sister and Mom plan the funeral while I was away. Sometimes you do not realize how divinely planned something is.

The day after he passed, I had a spa day in Whistler, BC while my hubby golfed. This is how we roll. This is our perfect day, and then we meet up for supper at night. This spa was so incredible, and I had been there before. The premise is hot, cold, rest. During a rest cycle, I found a hammock outside and jumped in. I was looking up at the sky and mountains and remembering all that had just unfolded days earlier. I started to cry. "Oh, gosh, please not the ugly cry in public at a silent spa," I begged my body. Tears rolled and rolled, and I soon realized my hammock was swaying. I stopped crying for a moment to check it and noticed there was no wind, and I was not moving the hammock. "What is going on?" I thought. I looked over at the other hammocks with people in them and they were as still as a stone. "What is happening? Is there an automatic button I pushed or what?"

I closed my eyes and saw my grandma on one side of me and my grandpa on the other. I felt like I was just a child in a cradle. They came to check in on me. Oh gosh, and the tears started up again, as I was swayed in this loving rock. This was such a beautiful moment for me and it's even hard to believe that happened. Why wouldn't it? Why can't it?

Our loved ones have just dropped off their aging bodies. Their spirit lives on forever, inside of us and possibly outside of us too. It's so hard to know what happens, but I look forward to seeing my grandparents in my dreams. I am thankful to have even more ancestors to call upon for help in this life. I feel so blessed.

Thoughts to Ponder:

1. How would you like to die? Short and sweet or a long drawn-out process?

2. Do you believe you have that option of how? Why or why not?

CHAPTER 26

TO NUMB OR TO PROCESS

It's 5am, the day of my grandpa's funeral. The air is misty, and the birds are already awake, singing their songs. I cannot sleep. I indulge in each minute of quiet to prepare me for the day ahead. This will be a super long day with family as we share and mourn together. I wish I was still sleeping and find myself as one who just wants to numb out of this experience. We miss a lot of growth when we numb out. How do we feel what we are feeling when we don't want to feel it?

I have two themed thoughts this morning. The first is that I just woke myself up from a literal nightmare. Someone was putting a needle in my arm as I slept so that they could get me to do something that I did not want to do. That is the theme to the Covid years, yet I feel it has some deeper meaning for me. I'm not sure if it is the government or religious force to obey and follow or if possibly there was some other trauma in my life when I was quite young.

This family gathering has brought in some players of the past and I just wonder how much subconscious memory is still in my brain. I had found some feelings awhile back that seem to have been related to a childhood trauma (maybe abuse) but I cannot pin point the event(s) or even talk myself into believing something actually happened. I am blocked. The mind and body are amazing with trauma. They only seem to show you what you can handle. They truly are our protectors.

When I first believed this was happening and it came into my awareness about a suppressed memory, it was all triggered by a nightmare. So why did I have one last night when it's been eight months since the last one? Is it from these people who are here for the funeral? Or am I just afraid to feel this day?

I strangely feel hungry, even though I never eat at 5am. I am never up at this hour. I usually begin to eat at about 11am. Food has always been my 'go-to!' It doesn't surprise me that I want to eat a large chicken dinner with chocolate cake and red wine right about now! It sounds so good to my body. That is typically what it reaches for when I am stressed or am unable to interpret feelings, thus being overweight. I must feel this. I will walk through this and hold myself back from driving to KFC at 5am! I'm sure they are not open, but wow that sounds so good to me. (I'm laughing at this right now!)

My other thought this morning is that of sadness. This too can be numbed by food. The sadness is over losing both my grandparents in less than a year. I'm not sure I realized their meaning until they had passed. These relationships grew into something beyond your typical grandparent relationship. For me, they were like the name says: second parents and oh so grand.

These last years with my grandpa have been cherished. He has been like a father figure to me. I would ask my grandpa for fatherly advice. We often talked about business, finances, politics, and what not. He heard my struggles in life, and I heard some of his. Our relationship was one million times deeper than that with my father. It was way more fun, too.

I feel like I got the best experience with this man. I had the best relationship, and yet, I bet even today at the funeral there would be people arguing with me that they had the best experience. It makes me wonder how can I make my life with others the best experience they have had?

I'm glad I woke up and am getting this out through writing. I even feel tired now. How amazing that once you express your feelings, you start to self-regulate. Journaling has always had this effect on me. If I would have had access to some chicken dinner (with mashed potatoes and gravy, skip the greens and load up a bun with butter), I would have missed this process. The next crisis would come along, and I would feel something within and be faced with the two choices again, numb or process. I am very good at numbing. Most of us are. We have so many ways to bypass feeling what we are really feeling.

Thoughts to Ponder:

1. What do you use as a distraction when you are feeling tough emotions? Food, business, alcohol, drugs, shopping, spending or something else?

2. What are your dreams/nightmares trying to say to you? Do you ever keep a record of them and try to figure out their meaning?

CHAPTER 27

ANCESTRAL TRAUMA

One of the best gifts I gave to myself for Christmas (yes, I buy myself Christmas gifts) was a subscription to Gaia TV. Just a couple weeks into my subscription, I came across a fascinating teaching all to do with generational trauma. In the 'woo woo' circles, we often talk about breaking the ancestral threads that our parents and grandparents may have passed down. These can be emotions of fear, hurt, shame or self-worth, self-esteem, self-love, etc. I had no idea that this was being studied and that scientists were hot on the trail to uncover something that we only believed to be true.

Enter Dr. Brian Diaz, a researcher who holds a Ph.D. in Psychiatry. He has a study with mice that is just fascinating in how it proves there is a generational affect to trauma.

With over 30 studies on PubMed, he is a well-respected doctor and researcher.

In one particular study, he had a scent that he introduced to a mouse and each time they went to smell it, they would receive a foot shock. This didn't harm them physically, but rather traumatized them. (For the record, I am not a fan of experimenting on animals, even mice.) He would do this to the mom and dad mice. Offspring of the father would then be tested by introducing this smell and they too would have traumatizing effects in their body, yet they were never literally traumatized. This went on for 6 generations. How is this even possible?

Why I bring this to anyone's attention is that it's so fascinating how science is catching up to what we thought and knew in our hearts. It is starting to prove these 'senses of knowing'. It's also fascinating in that, what is going on in our lives and what we deem as our little demons, may be coming from generations of trauma. We may also just be experiencing the trigger (the scent) and the action of the trauma is activated.

In my own life, I feel extremely fortunate to have had a great relationship with my grandparents, especially my mom's side of the family as you just read about. As I grew older, I could ask them some interesting questions and really get a sense of my ancestry.

Here is where things get so interesting.

I personally love wine and whiskey. I love feeling a little wine buzz and I could drink everyday if I didn't watch myself. I don't feel I am ever drunk, but I wouldn't want to drive after a couple glasses. My grandfather loved to drink. We talked about it often. He has two incredible stories about drinking. One was that he was denied access to World War II because of some physical issue due to drinking. The second interesting point about him was that my grandma was packed up ready to leave him, because he drank so much. She gave him an ultimatum: her, or liquor. He chose wisely and knew that choice changed his life.

Do you ever wonder where your 'bad' habits come from and why you do what you do? My dad, too I guess, was known for being a drinker and partier in his teens and twenties. Double whammy for generational desire to drink without really knowing why, and from both sides of my family.

What I would like to explore more here is the trigger as to what makes it happen. I know for myself, and asking the men in the family, the emotional reasons as to why we drink is not going to produce the outcome we truly desire. For myself, (whew it's getting raw and real… is it hot in here?) it's when I'm hurt, lonely, bored, celebratory, want to relax, angry…so pretty much all emotions?! Sometimes I just want to try a new bottle of wine and so I pour myself one. Sometimes I enjoy wine when I'm cooking and listening to music. Now you know why it's nearly every day! I wonder what my grandfather and dad were experiencing when they drank to a point of an ultimatum.

Think about your own life now. Are there things that you are stuck in? Could they be from generations prior?

I think about my mom and grandma regarding eating. I have known for quite some time that I was conditioned into the diet industry by these two. Looks and appearances were important and fat kids were not! There was always this struggle to watch your weight and what you ate. This was constant. Energy goes to what we focus on and so is it a surprise that I was the fat kid, that I struggle with my weight and must consciously try not to have food be my focus for the day? To me, this action was triggered by an emotion of self-worth. Worthiness for my grandma came from preparing food and serving it to her family and friends. That was my grandma's identity, a cook. My mom is very much the same as this was learned by watching. My mom added an element of reward for a hard day with food. She added treats and yet they always came with a condition. "Don't eat too many." "We shouldn't be having this, but…" "This has so much sugar and fat in it, but it's so good." It's almost like a reward and punishment through food. Again, likely a behaviour learned from her mom (my grandma) and I'm not sure how to trace it further back, but I find this all extremely interesting.

If I could ask my great grandparents why they ate or drank they may reply with, "Food was scarce, and we only ate to fuel our bodies". Drinking was likely illegal with prohibition, and when anyone tells us we can't do something, we usually do it! Alcohol was possibly drunk with secrecy and eating was eaten with scarcity. Well, no wonder I have tendencies to eat more than my body needs and for pleasure and to drink more often than I should. It's all making sense. We are fighting these demons that were programmed into us from our ancestors.

Our saving grace is acknowledging them. There are also many ways to start 'de-programming' our brains of these destructive ways. The more conscious the world becomes, the more these sometimes destructive ways will be eliminated. Some of the techniques I would suggest to de-program the brain include Hypnotherapy, Cognomovement, Somatic Release, Access Consciousness® and EMDR (eye movement desensitization and reprocessing therapy). There are likely more out there, but those are the ones that are coming to me at this moment. Sometimes just acknowledging this demon, will help to get it out.

[I want to add a side note here that this chapter was written nearly 4 years before it was published. Since then, my drinking has come to a near halt. It was a conscious choice and I replaced wine with other non-alcoholic drinks to break the habit at first. Then when I went back for a glass of wine, it just wasn't the same, and my body did not desire it. I found this so incredibly weird, and of course, I tested it a few times. This too was likely me breaking some ancestral pattern, as my life continues to do this. I am fascinated by it all: the history, the feelings associated, and the break in patterns. Now to do it with food; that will be my next break likely.]

This is worth exploring if you are stuck and wondering why you do what you do and feel what you feel. You may sabotage yourself with your decisions. Inquire with older family members or just take note if what you are dealing with is a sensitive subject. You are worthy to be free of these chains holding you back.

Thoughts to Ponder:

1. Do you have any destructive thoughts or behaviours that you are unsure of where they came from?
2. Have you observed any similar behaviours in your older family members?
3. Have you observed any of these behaviours being adopted by your children?
4. This is the experiment on mice if you would like to view:
   www.youtube.com/watch?v=STBN-LbQQgY

CHAPTER 28

YOU ARE LOVE

I continually get surprised by how, when I speak to people in their sessions with me, I often feel like I am speaking to myself. I guess I should quit being so surprised by this and accept that we are all one. One past client experience was no exception.

She arrived almost out of breath and took a seat in my trade show chair with a big exhale. She began telling me how lost she was feeling in the world and how people were causing her problems, and how she had so much in life yet still felt unhappy. I listened and asked my Higher Power how I could help this lady. I knew she was vulnerable, and I appreciated her honesty as I believe there are many people who feel exactly like her, either constantly or periodically.

This client was leaking power. She was giving it away to value others and possibly things as greater than her. When power is lost, we have nothing to create our own boundaries with. This is why it feels as though people are causing problems. When we are not all there ourselves (pieces of us are missing; power is lost). We may feel a deep unhappiness within us. Our soul is craving more of who we are, to feel complete, to feel the safety and satisfaction of being at home in our own life.

Why do we think someone else or even something else can provide us with what we are searching for?

What if we have everything we need within us rather than outside of us? Have we just forgotten how to provide for ourselves? It doesn't take long to get overwhelmed with advertising for the latest and greatest answer to your problems. What if YOU were the answer? What if it were that simple?

If you have a chance, read Matthew Perry's book *Friends, Lovers and the Big Terrible Thing: A Memoir.* As you know, Matthew played Chandler on the sitcom Friends. I loved this show and remember being so excited on Thursday nights when Friends was on. I feel like I grew up with these six people. I also watched their fame and fortune and thought, "Wow, they have it all." This was reiterated by reading Matthew's book. He did have it all and you know what, it wasn't enough. His soul was lacking the connection to itself, and he got lost in a world of drugs and alcohol. He admits he had everything and even dated some of the most beautiful, successful women in the world. He still was not happy. When he died his net worth was $120 million. Why was he not happy? He had everything. Would you be happy with $120 million, fame, pretty much any partner you wanted? We always think this is what we should be striving for; and yet, why do many who achieve it still struggle?

If you believe you come from Source and that Source is love, we then need to move back towards it. How can it be so simple yet so difficult? How does one love themselves? Well, how do you love others? You spend time with them, you care and nurture them, you listen to them, you encourage them, you hold them, soothe them, laugh with them, play with them – yes, it's that easy. Is it possible we become distracted by the worldly glam, glitter and busy-ness and forget this simple part of life?

Now for yourself, when was the last time you spent time with yourself, cared for yourself, nurtured yourself, listened to yourself, encouraged yourself, held yourself, soothed yourself, laughed at or with yourself or even played with yourself? (You can take that last bit however you want.)

When we honour and love ourselves the most in this world, the drama falls away. This may even include events, jobs or people. It can hurt to change, but not as much as going through life dishonouring or not loving everything about you! Satisfaction returns to us. We begin to feel complete, content and with a purpose.

I gently encouraged this lady from the trade show to come

back to herself. Yes, to make her life all about her. It sounds very selfish, but it is what will provide her with the energy and power to be able to look after others, out of love, should she choose.

If what I just wrote gives you the feeling of 'selfish', it likely isn't your feeling to begin with. Just have a look back at the ancestral line in your family and you will likely find it. You know, Jesus looked after himself first and then others. Think about all the times we read that he went away to learn or when he retreated alone to pray. This is nurturing the self. He did this so that he would have much to give to others. That is how it works.

When a person has figured this out, they are magnetic. They are so fun to be around. The exude this confidence as they do not have to prove themselves to anyone. When you love yourself deeply, you can love others deeply too. When you accept yourself, you can accept others. When you are kind to yourself, you are kind to others. When you have restored your energy, you have energy for others.

You will no longer see differences in other people. You just see other people making the best of their own world who may have different beliefs or choices in life than you, but they are just being them. Now imagine if the entire world would be able to think this way. We likely wouldn't have racism or wars, possibly even poverty or celebrity glorification. Just start with your own world, start with you, show your family and friends the way.

On the other side of the spectrum, you likely know people who are crusty and nasty to others. Maybe that's even you? These people are very hard on themselves. They do not love themselves as deeply as they can, and so they have a hard time loving and showing love, kindness, gentleness and even compassion to others. It's very possible that no one has shown them or taught them how. We all learn from what we see others do, especially others in authority when we are young. These crusty people constantly hold on to judgments and negative thinking. Everyone is wrong in their opinion; they are the only ones who are right. They have forgotten who they are, and it makes it impossible for them to give these attributes to others. They have swayed far, far away from the light of who they can be. They have forgotten where they came from.

If we all can spend some time getting to know ourselves, our power will return, our lights will get brighter, and we will feel close to the source. We will start to remember who we are and that we are part of creator, and the creator is love!

It's so simple yet complex, and possibly our lifelong mission to love ourselves and remember this while we are living! You are worthy of love. You are worthy of loving. You are worthy. You are love!

Thoughts to Ponder:

1. Who do you love the most on this planet? Love yourself as much and more than that. You will be

able to love them even deeper when you have mastered this love for yourself. Don't know where to start? Start by spending time with yourself. Get to know yourself as though you were a new friend.

Note: If you need help, I offer personalized private intuitive coaching and would love to show you this part of you that may be waiting to come and shine, and show you the way back to the real you: happy, content, and full of love.

CONCLUSION

Look a little deeper into life and in the struggle of the humanness you will find the spiritual bliss of who you really are. You will find you, an energetic, spiritual being having a human experience. When you die to the thought of your humanness, true living can begin. When you awaken to your energetic being, you can exist in this life knowing that it's only a temporary stop into something far beyond this worldly life.

Thank you for making it this far, in life ...and in my book. If I don't see you in this lifetime, I will see you on the other side.

OTHER RESOURCES

If you would like to get to know your energy more intimately, I invite you to check out my new online course. You will leave this course looking at energy in an entirely different way. This is a self-paced study, with a focus on becoming friends with your body, reading your body's energy, learning about the chakras and their main themes, how to disconnect from the energy of others, how to clear space and articles, a more in depth look at the 8th Chakra and so much more. Each module has a teaching video and a worksheet to apply the lessons. Check it out here:

It's All About Energy Online Course will provide many insights into your well-being. As a thank you for reading all this way, enjoy 20% off at checkout with the code: BOOK

I also offer personalized one on one Energy Coaching which you can explore here and see if it's the right fit for your life. There is opportunity to work with me for an hour or for a few months. I would love explore this world of energy with you.
https://www.carimoffet.com/intuitive-life-coaching

ACKNOWLEDGMENTS

I would like to thank my mom and dad for their care and influence on my life. Even though we do not see eye to eye on many topics in this book, I am thankful that we can still love and respect each other. In the end, that's all that matters.

Thanks to my husband, Craig, for putting up with my crazy stories. I knew when we were dating (a million years ago) that you were special, because you never laughed at all the weirdness that I experienced in life and still don't. You never shut off my superpower. I hope to never shut off yours.

Thank you, Fay Thompson, for one day listening to your gifts of editing and publishing. I'll never forget the phone call when I asked you what you did on the weekend, and you said you opened a publishing company. (Is that all?!) It has been super fun to do this with you!

I am so thankful for all the teachers and coaches I have had in my lifetime. Melinda Loo, you have kept me accountable to my gifts and offerings. Thank you for helping me push through the distractions, to share who I really am and to finally get this book published. You are a great coach and appeared at the perfect time in my life.

To the ten thousand plus people who had given me the privilege of working with them in some capacity through the years. It is because of you that I have grown in experience and have learned more about myself through your vulnerability and trust in me to serve you.

Lastly, I am going to thank a person who I never thought would ever be possible. I want to thank my ex-husband, Scott. (I know, this is weirdly crazy). If you were not brave enough to leave our marriage, not only would we have both been miserable but neither of us would have been able to find the path we were meant to travel. What looked like a complete disaster and heartache pivoted into the greatest blessing of my life and, likely, yours. I have told you this and now I tell the world because out of the chaos of destruction, emerges the most beautiful creation into who we are truly meant to be.

ABOUT THE AUTHOR

Cari Moffet uses her gifts and talents of massage therapy, energy work, essential oils, life coaching and meditation to relax and recharge a client's mind, body, and spirit. Cari has been in the alternative health field since 1996 and she loves guiding people to make choices to enhance their well-being in a natural way. She has numerous certificates in Massage Therapy, Life Coaching, Reiki, Medical Intuition, Meditation and more.

In 2019, Cari's first book entitled *It's All About Energy* became an Amazon #1 Best Seller in two categories. The book is a collection of stories to help people understand their own energy fields and body in a simple yet comprehensive way. *It's <u>Still</u> All About Energy* is a continuation of these teachings.

In her spare time, Cari enjoys traveling, playing piano, pottery, reading, paddling her kayak on the northern Saskatchewan lakes and spending time with family and friends.

Cari founded her company, Wholelife Wellness, in 2008 and has won a few awards in her community. She has been featured on Voice America talk radio and has written numerous magazine and newspaper articles.

Cari resides in Meadow Lake, Saskatchewan with her husband Craig and two fur babies, Wrigley and Fenway.

To work with Cari, book a session, or hire her for a speaking engagement, you can visit:

Website: www.carimoffet.com

Facebook: www.facebook.com/itsstillallaboutenergy/

Instagram: www.instagram.com/carimoffet

www.ingramcontent.com/pod-product-compliance
Lightning Source LLC
Chambersburg PA
CBHW071328120626
46546CB00002B/487
9781989840726